SHIP
CLERK TO
CEO

The Power of Curiosity, Will,
and Self Directed Learning

SHIPPING
CLERK TO
CEO

Ted Clark

DUDLEY COURT PRESS
SONOITA, AZ

Published in the USA by
Dudley Court Press
Sonoita, Arizona
www.DudleyCourtPress.com

Publisher's Cataloging in Publication Data

Names: Clark, Ted, 1953- author.

Title: Shipping clerk to CEO : the power of curiosity, will, and self directed learning / Ted Clark.

Description: Sonoita, AZ : Dudley Court Press, [2022]

Identifiers: ISBN: 978-1-940013-92-3 (paper) | 978-1-940013-93-0 (EBook) | LCCN: 2021938658

Subjects: LCSH: Clark, Ted, 1953- | Success in business--Handbooks, manuals, etc. | Success in business--Personal narratives. | Industrial management--Handbooks, manuals, etc. | Organizational change--Handbooks, manuals, etc. | Psychology, Industrial. | Consolidation and merger of corporations. | Curiosity. | Will. | Self-managed learning. |

BISAC: BUSINESS & ECONOMICS / Industrial Management. | BUSINESS & ECONOMICS / Mergers & Acquisitions. | BIOGRAPHY & AUTOBIOGRAPHY / Business.

Classification: LCC: HF5386 .C53 2021 | DDC: 650.1--dc23

Dudley Court Press is committed to publishing works of quality and integrity.
We are proud to offer this book to our readers.
The story, the experiences, opinions and words are the author's alone.
www.DudleyCourtPress.com

To my brother, Michael Scot Clark

CONTENTS

FOREWORD

Ted Clark's book *Shipping Clerk to CEO* is an inspiring read, outlining a straight-forward and well proven path to success that you won't get in a fancy MBA program. I should know, I graduated from Wharton and attended Harvard's CEO school. As CEO at H.B. Fuller, a $3 billion publicly traded company, I have known Ted for over 15 years and worked side by side with him as COO for the last four years. As partners, we've worked together to build greatness at H.B. Fuller. I've learned many lessons from him and have seen his advice in action through his words and deeds. He has impacted thousands of our employees and his book is a gift to anyone looking for proven advice on how to succeed in business (and in life).

Ted spells out a personal career model which says, "Anyone can do it". His 15 "lessons" including trust, networking, learning, and customer advocacy are all elements of his everyday approach to solving problems. These lessons have enabled him to grow our business, create followers, and mentor thousands of our employees. This is especially true as he drove sizable share gains and profit improvements during a flawless integration process wherein we maintained all key business leaders. H.B. Fuller purchased the company Ted built up as CEO for $1.575 billion; but it was Ted and his ability to lead with passion and purpose that has proven to be the most valuable asset.

Whether you've got a high school degree or an MBA from Wharton, you can learn from Ted and his book. I'm grateful to have worked alongside him and for all the lessons he's taught me. I'm so thankful that he wrote this inspiring, easy to read book so that many others can understand his story and success model.

—Jim Owens
President & CEO
H.B. Fuller Company

PREFACE

This is a book for dreamers and pragmatists alike, I believe.

It's a book for people in their twenties, or even high school, who are grappling with the tough decision about whether to invest in college or just jump straight into the workforce and earn that invaluable experience.

It's also a book for people midcareer who may be searching for inspiration to break through glass ceilings in spite of a lack of formal education.

It's a book meant to inspire workers of all walks, low level to high.

Now, I'm not the first CEO without a college degree, obviously. Ranked among the mightiest of the mighty are millionaires and billionaires who dropped out of college or never finished high school: Bill Gates, Steve Jobs, Michael Dell, Mark Zuckerberg. The list is an impressive who's who.

But you don't have to be born with the Midas touch to get into that elite club. Degree-free CEOs are even more widespread than you might imagine.

In the CEO Genome Project undertaken by ghSmart in 2018, which conducted in-depth surveys of 2,600 CEOs, a surprising 8% didn't complete college. And what they found among that subset of degree-less CEOs were three main similarities:

- They had become proven insiders who grew up in the industries where they now serve.

- They had achieved monumental results at each level of their rise; in other words, they got things done faster with fewer resources.

- And they had the ability to attract and retain talent.

Given that there are six million CEOs in the United States, statistically about 480,000 people are walking around as leaders of companies despite never having graduated college. That fact should be inspiring.

With the ever-growing costs of formal education and the endless information available for free online, it's easy to understand why more young people now see skipping school as a viable option.

In fact, the cost of college has tripled in the last twenty years, according to EducationData.org. Now hovering around $35,720 for an average four-year degree, higher education is a lavish pursuit that 75% of Americans believe is unaffordable and out of reach. As one of my great mentors would explain to me years later, the only real purpose of college is to simply open doors to higher-than-entry-level jobs. But that's all it does. A college degree *is* a head start, but you still have to learn everything about a job after that.

So, whether you're thinking of bypassing college because of poor grades, tight finances, lack of time, or pure disinterest, take heart in knowing a path to success without formal education is still available. We all start from somewhere.

I created this book to show the path that worked for me and one that should work for you, since I've highlighted the fundamental tenets of my success as actionable steps that can be replicated. My journey shows how achieving great career heights is possible despite nothing more than a couple of community college classes and years of hard work.

This book is a collection of the conscious choices I made every day along the way that compounded, one upon the other, to become the $240 million dollar global company I eventually came to head. I've shared as much detail as I could to show the connective tissue through my growing roles in leadership.

This book covers my early life and work experience along with my twenty-six years at Products Research & Chemical Corporation (PRC), where I rose from a shipping clerk with no college degree to the CEO of the company.

I also illustrate how I learned to build teams and manage people, set and meet objectives, and become a strategic thinker who gets things done.

Wherever I could, I sought mentors and great leaders who let me make my own mistakes and grow from them.

On these pages, I've identified the key lessons I learned through each phase of my career and highlighted those concepts throughout my personal story as themes and asides so the lessons are obvious and universal. Where possible, I added sidebars to further highlight the information I consider to comprise the pillars of good leadership.

It is my hope that my journey and its lessons inspire you.

LESSON 1

KNOW YOUR WHY

It's not enough to have lived. We should be determined to live for something.
—Winston S. Churchill

"People don't buy what you do; they buy why you do it."

That was the takeaway message from Simon Sinek's 2009 TED talk on the concept of WHY, which went on to become the third most watched video on TED.com with more than 54 million views.

This topic has become very popular in recent years as more people ask, "What is the magic potion that makes underdogs succeed? Why do some companies defy all assumptions and outperform more qualified competitors?"

Sinek speaks of leading from the inside, or from the heart, and points to Steve Jobs, Martin Luther King, and the Wright Brothers as examples of such leaders who inspired followers by appealing to the primal part of the brain that makes decisions based on emotions. The idea is that, when you share what rings as universal truth, you inspire others and win over followers.

We don't need to go into it here about how different hormones and neurochemicals produced in various regions of the brain affect emotional decisions, but let's just say the science involved in all this is quite interesting.

Dozens of books have been written on WHY and its importance as a driving force behind business success. After all, the right connections, money, and market conditions do not always equate to success, so investors and entrepreneurs are eager to better understand the formula behind synergy.

As an intuitive, gut-based decision-maker myself, I agree with Sinek's take. I think success comes down to the heart and soul of the people involved. When you remember what your purpose is and what your core beliefs are, you make the connections and decisions that bring about progress.

So, before you embark on decades of hours spent working for an employer, ask yourself, "Why? Why am I doing this?

Why do I get out of bed? What motivates me? What propels me forward, excites me, and makes me try harder?"

My Personal Whys

I was born on September 24, 1953, in Glendale, California, at Glendale Adventist Hospital to Eric and Laura Clark. A few days later, I went home to the place where I would spend the next nineteen years of my life—4943 Neola Place, Eagle Rock, a neighborhood just northeast of downtown Los Angeles.

Filled at the time with the families of policemen, firemen, city and county workers, as well as middle managers from the many manufacturing and distribution businesses in the area, Eagle Rock was a great place to grow up. The town was also populated with building and trades contractors, grips, cameramen, and other movie studio workers.

My dad worked as an accountant for Ducommun Metals and Supply Company, which was and still is the oldest publicly traded company in California, with roots back to the California Gold Rush. He was also the treasurer of the company's credit union, so between the two jobs, we were financially secure in our middle-class neighborhood.

So, if we're going to talk about WHYs and reasons to persevere, we should start with the rock in my family.

Dad

The survivor of a horrific accident, my dad's story is one of fortitude and achieving what we're told we never will. His tenacity strikes a deep chord with me and has at times played a part in propelling me forward. For this reason, I'm sharing his story here.

My dad was an only child who came to Los Angeles at a young age with my grandparents, who had initially been stationed off Vancouver with the British Royal Navy Signal Corps. Then, after my grandfather was discharged, the family settled into the Mount Washington area, a Los Angeles neighborhood known for its steep hills.

It was on one of these steep hills that my dad, around the age of ten, came barreling down, sitting on the handlebars of a friend's bike. As bad luck would have it, his foot got caught in the spoke of the front tire, and the bike suddenly lost control.

The accident mangled Dad's foot, ankle, and entire lower half of his leg. He described it as resembling hamburger meat.

He stayed in Los Angeles County General Hospital for six months. Fearful of gangrene, the doctors recommended amputating his leg, but my grandmother wasn't having that. She pushed back even though the word of a doctor in those days was nearly on par with that of God.

My dad prayed and pledged that he would never again say anything bad about anyone if God would spare him his leg.

The prayers and persistence, it seems, paid off. His leg was given a chance.

Sure, he experienced setbacks and infections, and when my dad did finally come home from the hospital, his one leg would ultimately be two inches shorter than the other.

That didn't stop him, though. Dad was competitive. He loved sports and exercise and being outdoors.

As he matured into a young man, even with a special shoe and walking with a slight limp, he stayed active.

He even went on to become a competitive tennis player, playing doubles in high school with then partner and future Wimbledon and US Open champion Bobby Riggs. He was also voted captain of the team and continued to play tennis well into his eighties.

And to his credit, Dad never did say anything bad about anyone. As a result, everybody liked him. He was engaging and had many friends—with not one vain bone in his body.

Even when his job was to repossess people's cars, Dad had a way of navigating difficult conversations and walking away respected.

He was a good father, too. He took me to work sometimes, where he was both an accountant and head of the credit union, a place he spent forty years of his life.

When he brought home work, like inventory cards, he made sure to expose me to the lesson by asking me to help add up the numbers on a mechanical adding machine to double-check his calculations. He also taught me tennis and discipline and pointed out key life lessons, like to make sure the person you're learning from is better than you. The lesson centered around tennis at the time but certainly resonates through every facet of life, especially business.

So, maybe I get some of my tenacity from my father, from knowing the tragic hurdles he himself had to overcome, but I definitely get some from my mom, too.

Mom

It's hard not to grow up ambitious with a mom like mine. She was the kind of strong-willed cheerleader who tells you that you can be the president someday.

Mom lived for us kids and, thanks to my dad's two jobs, she could stay home to raise my older brother, Mike, and me until I was old enough for her to work part time. Mike was seven years older due to two miscarriages Mom suffered before I was born.

With Scottish roots and a well-educated pharmacist for a dad, my mom grew up slightly affluent. Her dad started his own pharmacy and had three branches and a pharmacy school. The Great Depression, though, forced him to cut back to one location, humbling the family to middle class and imprinting a heightened awareness of class consciousness within my mom.

She would have liked to go on to college, but life didn't offer her that chance. After a short stint at a pharmacy and then a bank, she got married.

Though she wrestled with her own status in the world, to her credit, she never once pressured my brother or me to go to college. She considered it a personal decision and was supportive of whatever choices we made. I could do whatever I wanted, which was quite liberating. She trusted us to find our own way.

Perhaps the story that sticks with me the most about my mom, and which I believe impacted my young psyche profoundly, is the one about her purse.

When I was about nine years old, I liked to run down to the corner store near our house, and so, like most kids, I was always asking for money. My mom, in her wise ways, would direct me to where her purse was hidden in the closet and grant me permission to take from her wallet the amount I felt I needed.

"Take what you want; put back what you don't need," she'd say. She called this the "freedom of the purse." Now, my mother was not naïve. She was an intuitive woman, the kind who wouldn't hesitate to give you the eagle-hawk look if she caught you lying. I have to confess, I took a little more out of her wallet than I needed. But this reverse psychology lesson of hers worked its magic on me because after about a week or two, my conscience couldn't let me continue. I knew she needed that money for food and bills. It just wasn't right. I felt selfish.

That lesson in trust is one that stays with me today. When you give people responsibility, as opposed to telling them what to do, you find more often than not that people will rise to the occasion. Yes, some will let you down, but usually, people will do the right thing, and this is the basis upon which trust is built.

I always start with the assumption that people are good. I get that from my mom.

My Brother

For all the lessons my mom and dad taught me, however, none has left a more indelible mark on my psyche than that of my brother Mike's fleeting life.

He is the reason I wake up and the person who most prominently altered the course of my life. The biggest events in my young life revolved around him.

I not only admired my brother, I idolized him. He was smarter than I was. He understood concepts, such as mechanical stuff, better than I did.

Smart with many friends, Mike was cool in the Steve McQueen sort of way. Quiet and thoughtful, he was a hands-on guy with the mind of an engineer. He understood how to fix things. He would take apart engines and watches just to put them back together.

He started building hot rods and got into the drag racing scene. He bought a 1958 Chevy Impala and customized it with a 409 Chevy engine with dual four-barrel carburetors. Then he added a four-speed Hurst transmission and limited-slip rear differential. To that, he had added drag racing tires while somehow keeping it all street legal (or at least close to it).

On Saturday nights, Mike and his friends would caravan out to the old Fontana drag strip to drag race. He came home with a lot of trophies. Although I was too young to go too, I was in awe of all the racing stories.

My brother was clearly held in high esteem by his peers and was a natural, charismatic leader in his group of friends.

•••

By the early '60s and with the Vietnam War in the news daily, Mike joined the navy reserve. He did his basic training at the Navy Reserve Center in Chavez Ravine near Dodger Stadium in LA.

After that, he was called up to serve on a dry dock doing maintenance and repair work at the US Navy base in Subic Bay in the Philippines.

His deployment was tough on our family—especially my mom. Mike would be away for that whole year. Honestly, it seemed way longer than that to me. We would get letters from him, and occasionally he would send locally made gifts for us.

His duties consisted of sandblasting and painting ships in dry dock. In particular, he was assigned to get the aircraft carrier USS Forrestal back to sea.

The Forrestal is the carrier that the late Senator John McCain served on as a flight officer. Sadly, it had an ordnance accident that caused a massive explosion and fire in which 134 sailors died and 161 were injured, including McCain. That was one of my brother's last missions for the navy.

When he returned home, I had just turned fifteen. I was excited to see him, but we noticed that Mike had lost a lot of weight and had a dry, persistent cough. Something was clearly wrong.

My mom took him to the doctor, who took many X-rays. Initially, the doctor diagnosed him with drunkard's lung—normally found in alcoholics who slept in the street on their sides and fluid would accumulate in one lung. Mike immediately challenged that diagnosis, as he was not a heavy drinker.

After more doctors' visits, Mike finally got a biopsy of one of his lungs. The diagnosis: cancer. Mike's cancerous lung was removed, which led to the darkest day of my life before or ever since.

When I came home from school on that day of the surgery, my mother was sitting near the fireplace with the minister from our Episcopal church. *Something must be terribly wrong*, I thought.

My mother explained that Mike's cancer had spread beyond his lung and that he had been given a year to live. This hit me so hard, I could not speak, could not cry, and could not move. I simply could not process *anything* about it, and still cannot to this day. Honestly, I'm not sure I ever will.

We later found out that while the cancer was detected in his lungs, it had started as melanoma, a skin cancer that had spread to his organs.

When my brother recovered enough to come home from the hospital, he never complained or felt sorry for himself.

To his credit, Mike decided to live life to the fullest as long as he was able.

His buddies would come over, pick him up, and take him to the races and other places, even as he continued to lose weight and have an increasingly difficult time getting around.

Mom quit her part-time job to be with him as much as possible. She would take him fishing at the Santa Monica pier and do other activities, just to be with him.

Mike began to treat me as more of an equal than a little brother. We'd have long talks, and he'd show me how to work on cars, which he loved doing until almost the end. Although we knew it was coming, we all still felt the shock when, almost a year to the day from his diagnosis, Mike passed away.

Even when you know someone is terminal and especially when you are young, you hope against hope that the outcome will somehow be different.

Nobody in our family got therapy to help us deal with Mike's death. It just wasn't the kind of thing that that generation did. Even within the family we did not speak of it much; the subject was too painful to bring up, especially around my mother, who suffered in silence. That was just the way it was done. When my grandparent immigrated to the United States, they left their families behind and everything they knew in the UK, never to see them again. In the British culture they came from, people in my family simply carried on.

My mother took my brother's death hard and was never the same after that. She would stay up late, sleep late, and lived with a discernible sadness through the rest of her life.

Dad suffered badly too, but did not show it as much as Mom. I think he felt he had to pick up the pieces of our family and get us moving forward again.

More easy-going in nature, Dad was able to keep our life stable, but Mom, tough as she was, had sharp edges with highs and lows, making her a bit unpredictable. She still looked out for the family, had a good sense of humor, and was well liked by her friends, but sadness always lurked below the surface.

I think watching my mom endure such a horrible loss made me more sensitive in dealing with other people. I would sometimes think of my mom and then take into account the suffering that some people experience, which informed how they viewed life. That perspective has always helped me to soften my approach.

As for me, at age fifteen, I could not deal with Mike's death. Part of me wanted to avoid the reality, go on, and not think about the pain. For years, I would dream about him and imagine that he had never left.

Another part of me wanted to make sense of it all.

In the end, all I could come up with is that I needed to figure out a way to *live a life for both myself and my brother* as if he stilled lived on through me.

How would I do this? I didn't know, but this goal has been on my mind ever since.

Death: The Ultimate Why

Steve Jobs summed it up nicely in his Stanford University commencement speech when he said, "Remembering that you are going to die is the best way I know to avoid the trap of thinking you have something to lose."

Mike's death changed me. Maybe it made me braver. Maybe it made life more urgent. But this is probably true for anyone who loses someone close.

When we see someone else's life end, we gain a greater perspective that helps us appreciate the present and be less distracted by the unessential. That experience colors everything. It makes us kinder and pushes us to assert a lasting impression in life—to show up, be seen, and add value.

Perhaps it *is* the very knowing that we will die that best sets the scene for how we live. The impermanence of life is, after all, what makes it so precious.

Take time to figure out why you do what you do, and I believe you'll find everyday tasks easier and easier.

LESSON 2

NETWORK

*Networking is marketing. Marketing yourself, marketing
your uniqueness, marketing what you stand for.*
—Christine Comaford

I heard an industry expert on an NPR segment a few years ago proclaim that at least 70%, if not 80%, of jobs are never posted or publicly advertised.

Think about that. That means *most* positions are being filled purely through referrals and word of mouth. That's a fascinatingly high number of hidden opportunities, and the practice happens all around the world.

In a global survey of almost 16,000 LinkedIn members across seventeen countries, 70% said they were hired in 2016 through a connection at the company. And 80% felt that networking drove promotions and success.

This data proves once again that getting a job really is all about who you know. The statistics also reveal how much people are creatures of habit and lean toward risk aversion whenever possible. We like to know what we're getting into.

And that's what hiring managers want most: character references. They want to know your interpersonal capabilities as well as your overall disposition. Does this person have integrity? Is he ethical? What's his judgment like? Will she be ambitious, funny, and respectful or will she complain and talk behind others' backs? These are details a resume can't disclose.

When someone goes out of their way to pick up the phone and suggest you for a job or to hand deliver your resume to their boss, that shows the hiring employer up front that you are worth their time, that you have a way with people and a personality that's agreeable.

A reference takes much guesswork out of the hiring process. Trust takes time to build, and by having people who will vouch for you, you save the employer time in calculating whether you will be a bad hire.

For young people, the experience conundrum is typically the biggest hurdle they have in landing a first job. It's that Catch-22: Nobody will hire you without experience, but you can't gain experience without being hired.

This is why the power of networking becomes evident so early on in people's careers. A simple referral can sometimes take you further than any education or previous experience can.

So, if almost every good job out there is hidden from sight until you're in the six degrees of separation web, how do you get in?

Perseverance

In a LinkedIn survey, 35% of respondents said that a casual conversation through LinkedIn Messaging led to a new opportunity.

So, there's one answer: technology. Another way to make a connection is through industry events and conventions to put ourselves face-to-face with potential mentors and partners.

The lesson here, however, isn't about swapping business cards. I'm talking about relationships and the art of turning strangers into friends and allies. Networking isn't just a side activity involving emails. It's every smile and handshake you extend throughout the day.

The easiest way to grow your network is to take the time to build genuine relationships on a daily basis. You never know who that stranger is going to turn into for you. Over time, relationships evolve. Someone you know now may become a future mentor and you don't even realize it.

Want to break into a certain industry? Shadow a family friend around the office for a couple of days. See if they will refer you for a job or an internship or write you a letter of recommendation for college. The process starts with having the guts to ask and say yes to opportunities. Accept invitations. Go to parties. Exchange information.

When the time comes to search for work, you can tap into those connections for referrals, insights, job leads, and other valuable information. Let them know that you are available for them in the same way.

In my case, I was just a kid who needed a job and I had a friend who helped get me there, but that's how everything starts, right?

Moving On

A line in a song by the band Twenty One Pilots talks about being inspired by death. Maybe I experienced a little of that.

Watching the breakdown of my brother's body made me want to use my energy, youth, and strength to go out and live my life fully while I still could. I couldn't fix my brother, but I could do the things that he could not.

As such, my life slowly began to normalize around school, sports, and girlfriends.

Academically, I had done well in elementary school and junior high school, but I lost focus in high school and didn't do so well in math and science. I did enjoy social studies and history, however, and got good grades in them.

I was also on the swim team and participated in other sports such as skiing. I liked socializing, too, but my main goal (shared by almost all my friends) was to get my driver's license at age sixteen. It was the ultimate ticket to independence in California's car-obsessed culture.

Nurture Your Network

Who you know and what they think of you matters. People have always gotten fast-tracked into jobs and promotions, thanks to relationships.

Learning how to connect with people is one of the best skills you can build for a prosperous career.

Some people are natural "connectors," as Malcolm Gladwell describes in his book *The Tipping Point: How Little Things Can Make a Big Difference*. These are charismatic people with one hundred or more connections in their network, who frequently introduce people and cross-pollinate ideas between groups.

There are books upon books out there that teach the art of networking, but I'll drop a few of my own suggestions here:

Go for quality over quantity. List your professional goals and strategize who can help you get there. Be clear about who you want to connect with. Don't just collect cards. Seek mutual friends on social media to try and establish an organic connection. Third-party endorsements give you credibility.

Schedule time to network. For relationships to grow, you need to check in on those contacts on a regular basis. Set aside time for networking each week. Build it into your schedule, and prioritize who you should be following up with first. Make yourself likable before promoting your professional strengths.

Give first, then receive. Make yourself of service to new contacts before asking for favors. Prematurely tapping a source for help is a major mistake in networking. It can turn contacts cold that could have eventually been a boon for you. See if you can connect people within your circles in a useful way first. Do research on your contact to understand how you can be of service, and focus on what you have in common to build rapport.

Overcome your fears. If you are an introvert, challenge yourself to try a little harder at each event. Talk a little longer or to more people. Rehearse for it like you would a job interview, prepping yourself with potential topics of discussion.

Follow up. Continued interactions strengthen relationships and keep you in the forethought of their minds for when opportunities do present themselves. Thank people, let them know you have them in mind, or send along industry articles or updates that pertain to previous conversations.

So, on my sixteenth birthday, my mom took me to the DMV. I took the test in our Datsun 510 and passed with flying colors.

After that, she let me take the Datsun to school. I still remember feeling the freedom on that first day with a car. Driving reminded me of my brother—the way he must have felt all those times driving on his own. Maybe that was him watching over me.

A Foot in the Door

I suppose the motivation to buy my *own* car was what pushed me to find that first after-school job.

Searching for a job was a daunting task, though. I felt shy around adults, and the idea of cold calling businesses to ask for a job was something I dreaded.

Fortunately, I learned the power of networking.

Over the years, several older guys on my street had worked as delivery boys for Brogan's Drugstore. Eddie Garren was the current one to have that job, and he would soon graduate from high school and move on to other things.

So, as luck would have it, Eddie recommended me to Ed Lewinter, the owner of Brogan's, and Ed agreed to interview me.

The interview went smoothly. Ed asked if I had a driver's license and a car that was insured. Yes, I did—and because Eddie had recommended me, I was hired. Easy as that.

Ed was a great boss who only required that I arrive on time and treat our customers with respect. My route included seven retirement hotels and convalescent hospitals, along with regular family homes and apartments.

Most of our customers were elderly and retired, so dealing with them required patience. Many were lonely. They looked forward to my arrival and wanted to talk.

I had to plan my time so I could be friendly and respectful while getting the rest of my deliveries done on time.

I loved every minute of the job. While at the drugstore, I helped manage the inventory as well as count pills and dispense drugs under Ed's guidance.

Ed's assistant, Monette, was only a few years older than me, but she was more mature and took an interest in training me to do the more mundane tasks and keep me busy.

When I started, I used my mom's car until I could save up for my own. At that point, Dad's treasurer job at the credit union worked in my favor. He came home one night and told me he had repossessed a Honda 305 motorcycle. Knowing that it would be perfect for my delivery job, I bought the bike a few days later.

The flaw in his plan was that my mother had not been made aware until after the transaction happened. This created a dilemma for Dad, who ended up in Mom's doghouse for some time. As for me, I could not have been more thrilled.

The little Honda was a real workhorse. I rode it to school and used it for work. Everything was going great until one day a small dog ran out in front of my bike, and I ended up on the side of the road.

This became even too much for Dad, and I ended up selling the bike for a small profit. A friend of mine was selling his Ford van, so I bought that, knowing it would work even better for making deliveries.

Meanwhile, at school, our counselors were emphasizing that we take college preparation courses such as calculus, algebra, biology, and other advanced studies.

I had made it a practice to avoid advanced classes. I only wanted to take the ones I needed to get a diploma, and I knew I could learn something useful in shop.

My main interests at the time ran toward having fun in extracurricular activities, especially work and sports.

In truth, I wasn't thinking too far ahead; I just wanted to fill my time with activities I enjoyed and did well.

Mike still weighed heavily on my mind, so I took it easy on myself. By my senior year, I had become a good skier and that, along with work and dating, was my principal interest.

•••

As for Brogan's Drugstore, I have fond memories. All in all, this first job gave me a tremendous amount of confidence to be around adults and elderly people.

I loved it so much that I ended up staying there for almost two years—until I graduated high school.

This simple lesson is worth repeating: Put yourself out there. We all know enough people to get us to where we want to go.

Lessons Learned at the Bottom

Here are some of the early lessons I learned about work from my younger years:

Say yes. Be open to opportunities and willing to learn. Take on all the responsibility you can, no questions asked. It's the fastest way to grow.

(continued on page 21)

Volunteer. Do tasks not assigned to you. Keeping busy with many tasks helps otherwise mundane jobs feel more meaningful and gets you noticed by management. And regardless of what your co-workers are doing, always try to do your best.

Seek mentors. An old saying goes that the mentor appears when the student shows himself to be ready and eager. I think there's something to that. When you keep your eyes open to learning opportunities, they tend to present themselves.

Anticipate needs. Try to do a task before someone has to ask you. Perceiving the bigger picture and understanding how the steps of the entire process work pave the way for promotions.

Think on your feet to close deals. Go into meetings prepared to pitch from the top of your head. That means, do your research in advance, anticipate questions, and understand your clients' needs. You'll be more confident when making your off-the-cuff pitch if you've done your homework.

Be early. I've heard it said that five minutes early is on time, on time is late, and late is not acceptable. That's how I was raised, and this mindset always served me well.

Respect your boss. Every employee is expendable. I've seen plenty let go from lack of discipline or for being mouthy. Treat people how you want to be treated. You may one day find your boss defending you in front of a rude customer.

Speak up. Don't be afraid to share what's on your mind. Everyone has a different set of skills to offer. Don't let your age stop you from offering up ideas in a meeting. Sometimes the young minds have the best ideas.

Mirror your boss. Employees should make an effort to mimic their boss's communication preferences, both in mode and frequency. Some people prefer face-to-face updates, but for others, email, text, or written reports may be better. You should be direct and ask your supervisor how they prefer updates and how often.

LESSON 3

DIVERSIFY

Diversification and globalization are the keys to the future.
—Fujio Mitarai

Many of us grew up learning contradictory parables about risk, such as, "A bird in the hand is worth two in the bush"—meaning, be content with what you have; don't risk it all by venturing for more.

Then we hear something like, "Don't put all your eggs in one basket"—totally the opposite advice.

Advice can be confusing, but as I've gotten older, I see how important it is to hear all of these conflicting lessons to remind us that balance is always key in life, and the truth is somewhere in the middle.

I mention this because there are some strong camps around the idea of diversifying in business. Warren Buffett, for example, has been very vocal against it, saying: "Diversification is a protection against ignorance. [It] makes very little sense for those who know what they're doing."

Warren Buffett is famous for his "circle of competence," which offers the idea that investors should identify what they're most knowledgeable about and focus specifically in that direction.

Doubling down on that point, Buffett's business partner Charlie Munger famously added: "Nobody wants to go to a doctor that's half proctologist and half dentist."

You can also find many articles online with reasons to stay focused in business. Specializing in one product creates production efficiencies and builds a stronger brand.

One way to avoid mediocracy is to stop trying to be all things to all people. Instead, imprinting one's mark on a narrow segment of the market can be easier.

From that perspective, diversification is not the right path for every business. However, there are different ways to define diversity in business and various reasons for it.

In general, diversifying is an approach for more rapid growth. Typically, a company will seek to diversify once its existing product or market no longer offer opportunities to expand. In large corporations, diversification often happens because of pressure from investors.

In some ways, diversifying can be seen as a transitionary phase of adapting. As the consumer needs change, businesses must put out feelers into more viable markets through the development of brand-new products and services.

Modifying and upgrading existing formulas and services can be another—less risky, less expensive—way to reach new markets.

Applied mathematician and businessman Igor Ansoff, the "father of strategic management," back in 1957 declared diversification to be one of the four basic management strategies behind growth—the others being: product development, market development, and market penetration.

He noted that diversifying can be risky compared to other strategies because of all the unknowns in uncharted territories. For starters, it diverts financial and personnel resources away from the core industry, and the further away you get from your core market, the more risk you run into.

But done well—once the original business is stable and successful—diversifying can turbocharge growth.

In the later stages of my own career, I would learn a lot about diversification, particularly in "vertical diversification," which is sometimes called vertical integration. That's where a company moves up or down the supply chain by merging two or more stages of production, usually operated by unrelated companies.

This chapter, though, focuses on a simple lesson I learned early in my working life: Diversifying isn't just one of the pillars of business growth; it's also necessary for business survival, specifically when it comes down to customer diversification.

I know today that having any one customer comprise more than 50% of a business is a big risk; in fact, more than 10 to 12% gets risky, but of course, that depends on the industry.

There's a rule of thumb in business—the 80/20 rule, or the Pareto principle—that suggests that 80% of a company's sales typically come from 20% of its customers.

Larger corporations can sometimes manage the risk of huge customer concentrations, but even then this scenario is not ideal.

Anyway, this is a lesson I was about to learn.

A One-Man Show

In the summer of 1971, I graduated from Eagle Rock High School with no plan for what to do next. I did not have the grades nor the right courses to get into a four-year college. My options were to find a job or attend a junior college.

At that time, a small percentage of high school graduates went to college while many sought good jobs at the phone company, one of the new cable companies, or the bank branches. Some planned to test for civil service jobs. Many entered the trades as apprentices in plumbing, electronics, and carpentry. Still others applied for work in manufacturing and logistics. Some joined the military or were drafted if they had low draft lottery numbers.

After graduation, I continued to work part time at the drugstore and otherwise enjoyed the summer at the beach or swimming in my parents' backyard pool. In the evenings, I hung out with friends, went to parties, and socialized. We could buy beer at certain liquor stores that were loose with the rules of selling only to people over twenty-one—you know, the things kids do when finding their identity. I needed time to regroup.

At the end of summer, I knew I had to either go to junior college or get a full-time job, so I asked myself, *What would Mike have done?*

I like to think that some of my intuition comes from my brother, but true or not, I had a strong impulse to jump straight into work, so I followed it.

I applied for a job that I found in the classified ads, interviewed, and was hired. Like that, I became the new inventory clerk and general assistant at Alexander Auto Headliner Company in East Los Angeles.

Mr. Alexander, the owner, was an entrepreneur who had started the business out of the back of his car.

In the late 1950s, he had the idea to provide replacement headliners to auto upholstery shops. He started by visiting used car lots and measuring the headliners—interior fabric roof liners—for different makes and car models. Then he made patterns that he kept for future orders.

Until then, auto upholstery shops had to custom-make replacement headliners in their shops. That would take a long time and increase the overall cost of the job. Mr. Alexander called on the upholstery shops to promote his new service, and they soon began to order from him. He actually sewed the headliners in his garage himself!

Over time, he developed a thriving business in replacement headliners and auto upholstery cloth and fabrics. He added other auto accessories such as side body molding and precut and sewn landau tops, which were popular in the '60s, '70s, and early '80s.

Recognition Motivates

In my interview with Mr. Alexander, he made two things clear to me. First, he would pay $2.40 an hour, and I should not expect a raise. He considered this a starting job for young people. Most only stayed for about a year to gain experience and then they'd apply for higher paying jobs. All that was fine with him.

Second, he expected a full day's work, and I needed to take orders from the ladies who cut and sewed the headliners and landau tops. I had to make sure they had the right rolls of material for the right job at the right time, and after the job was complete, I had to return the remaining material into inventory.

This task seemed simple enough until I found out each roll of fabric weighed up to fifty pounds and was about five feet long. To move a roll manually, it had to be lifted onto my shoulder, carried to a sewing table, and mounted onto a horizontal pole.

From there, the cloth could be pulled out onto a large cutting table where the ladies used a pattern to cut the material before taking it to the sewing stations.

About ten ladies and tables had to be serviced with up to ten roll changes a day with only one or two people doing the changes.

After a day of this, I was physically exhausted. *This is probably why no one stayed more than a year*, I thought.

Doing this work, I quickly got stronger. As I mastered this move, I was asked to help get orders set up for shipment and also to assist our walk-in customers. I enjoyed the work and the people, especially the ladies, and I thrived in the nine-to-five structure.

To escape boredom, I volunteered for any tasks that came up and developed ways to make the work interesting and diverse. As an example, I made it my business to ensure that once a roll needed changing, I would do it right away so the ladies never had to ask for a change.

I would survey the work area and do other tasks, keeping it my main priority to make sure the rolls were always where they should be without being asked. The ladies loved that, and my work really impressed Mr. Alexander.

After about six months, I was rewarded for my hard work when Mr. Alexander broke his own rule and gave me a ten-cent-an-hour raise. He said I was the best worker he had hired to date and that the ladies on the sewing tables were my biggest supporters. "Keep up the good work," he said.

I felt good to be recognized in this way. It was not the money but his recognition alone that motivated me.

Opportunities Born from Relationships

While working at Alexander's, I got to know some of the guys in their early twenties who had started their own businesses installing vinyl side body molding on cars. They purchased the side body molding from Alexander Auto Headlining.

In those days, cars did not come from the factory with any moldings to protect the doors from scratches and dents when people got in and out of their cars. The molding, made by 3M, was sold as an aftermarket product.

Mr. Alexander developed and made small plastic chrome-plated end pieces to give the molding a professional finish. They looked like little chrome arrows at each end of the molding.

Workplace Recognition

As a leader I've seen positive feedback unlock potential in people. I've seen it inspire innovation, too. We always think better when we feel that the people around us are supportive, don't we?

I've always prided myself on seeing the humanity in my team and recognizing their hard work well done.

When I look back on lessons I learned at my first job out of high school, I'd say this: this first moment of being recognized at work was an important validation for me. It's a reminder today that sometimes showing gratitude is as easy as a pat on the back and a ten-cent raise.

Be it a thank you, an apology, or a congratulations, tokens of appreciation and respect for coworkers and employees, no matter how subtle, add up. Sometimes they are the glue that holds a job together.

Companies call it employee recognition—or social recognition to include the peer-to-peer culture—and studies have shown that the more gratitude employees get, the better they perform. For starters, appreciation makes people happier, which in turn motivates them, boosting their engagement and productivity and promoting collaboration.

Public recognition also sends a message to other employees about what success looks like, reinforcing loyalty. It inspires innovation, too, by validating feelings of job mastery.

Validated employees are also more loyal and less likely to quit. In one study published by IBM, the intention to quit one's job was twice as high among employees who didn't receive recognition—51%—compared to those who did—25%.

To market this molding product, he helped young entrepreneurs set up mobile side-body installation businesses by training them on installation methods and providing credit.

The mobile installers usually had a van or truck to carry inventory of the different colored moldings and chrome tips along with a simple set of installation tools.

They would start by cold calling sales or service managers

at new and used car dealerships to sell the molding and their installation service. Many succeeded in making good money doing this.

After about ten months working for Mr. Alexander, he approached me and asked if I wanted to start my own installation business. He would provide credit and let me use an office desk to make calls. He would also provide leads through his contacts in the auto industry.

I honestly could not believe my luck. *I had an opportunity to start my own business at eighteen years of age!*

I accepted, of course, and within a month, I had started the Clark Mobile Molding Company that I ran from the back of my van.

When I went to Bank of America to set up a business checking account, I remember the manager treating me well and showing curiosity about how I would run a small business.

She would be the first of hundreds of bankers I would eventually meet, and she's still my favorite. I opened my first account with a $50 deposit.

Of Eggs and Baskets

My first order of business was to sell to potential customers— and I wasn't very good at it. I was shy. I had no skills or training in sales, and the car dealer sales and service managers I approached intimidated me.

My pitch was terrible, but by using the leads provided by Mr. Alexander, I did manage to get work at a few local car dealerships. In the first couple of months, I had secured five dealers as customers.

Once that happened, the rest was relatively easy. The dealers would call and ask for an installation on a certain day and time. I'd arrive, pick up the purchase order from the sales or service manager, do the installation, send a bill at the end of the month, and wait for a check.

I was earning more than my wages at Alexander Auto Headlining but not by much *until* Mr. Alexander gave me a lead for Ralph Williams Ford in Cerritos, California. At the time, it was the world's largest Ford dealer.

Throughout Southern California, Ralph Williams was a legendary car salesman and pitchman who appeared on TV daily. He would pitch the cars on his lot with a TV camera trailing him, selling and financing them using the theme, "Always great cars, low pricing, and low or no-money-down financing." He'd put every family in a reliable car or truck that "fit [their] lifestyle."

This special lead turned into a big opportunity. I arranged an appointment with the sales manager to see what he was looking for so I could make a proposal.

The gregarious, fast-talking sales manager, Tony, was dressed in a white sports coat, blue slacks, and white shoes. I was dressed in jeans, a tee shirt, and tennis shoes. I had long hair and looked younger than my eighteen years. Quite an odd couple.

When I asked what he needed, he walked me out to the massive used car lot that was several blocks long. He put his arm around my shoulder and pointed to the cars on the lot. Then he said, "I want you to put molding on every single car on this lot. We park them close together so we can sell volume every day, and we have a lot of issues with door dings. We need to protect these cars so we can sell them as fast as we can. Dings are a problem for us."

He then asked me for my price. I got the feeling he didn't want a written proposal, that I had to name a number on the spot to close the deal, so I gave him one I thought would be competitive and told him I could start the next day.

To my surprise, he immediately agreed then took me to the finance manager, who gave me purchase orders for the next day. The lot had between three hundred and four hundred cars, and the salesmen moved them as fast as they could.

I was asked to put molding on ten to fifteen cars a day, or fifty to seventy-five a week. I was to come to the lot every day at seven a.m. and do as many cars as I could by twelve noon.

Then they'd get the cars washed and ready by late after-noon when Ralph Williams would come out and film his famous daily live commercial.

I was making more money in a month than I had in six months working for Alexander Auto Headlining. For the nine months leading up to the end of summer of 1972, things were going great. In fact, the work at Ralph Williams Ford was so lucrative, I dropped my other dealers.

Being young, inexperienced, and making oodles of money, I spent afternoons with my friends either around a pool or at the beach. Life was good. And I knew Mike would approve.

Until one day, I showed up at Ralph Williams Ford and the sales manager broke the news.

Williams had been indicted for fraud. The world's largest Ford dealer was being taken over by his rival, Cal Worthington, another famous car dealer in Southern California.

Cal was well-known for his live television commercials that opened with an announcer saying, "Here's Cal Worthington and his dog Spot!"

But "Spot" was never a dog. Spot was sometimes a live tiger or a seal or an elephant or a chimpanzee or a bear—but never a dog.

After his introduction, Cal Worthington would use essentially the same pitch that Ralph Williams had done. And like Williams, he became a local legend. With this merger, he rose in stature to be the undisputed king of the auto dealers in Southern California.

Unfortunately for me, Cal Worthington had his own side-body molding guy, so I went out of business overnight. In less than a year, my new enterprise had failed.

I knew right away that I had messed up. You need more than one customer to run a business.

I learned many lessons from this early failure, especially the dangers of customer concentration—don't ever put all your eggs in one basket.

All this knowledge would come in handy later.

The Importance of Diversifying

It's business 101. Don't put yourself at the mercy of only one client. Spread the risk around. It's a philosophy that should carry over through investment, finance, and business.

When your business is young, diversifying can simply mean building in alternative income sources, such as adding landscaping, tree trimming, and turfing to a lawn-care service.

Some companies move into unrelated industries for a bigger financial cushion in case there's a sudden burst in their core business market.

As businesses grow, diversification gets more complicated and sometimes involves buying up competitors or suppliers to increase market share or improve synergy.

When branching off from a core business, it's important to venture out in stages.

Here are some important considerations:

- Seasons can cause problems for businesses; be sure to diversify seasonal services and product offerings to guarantee steady work flow year-round.

- Focus on value for the customer. What is a service or product they need or use every day or every week as opposed to occasionally?

- Be an expert in the market. Build on your strengths as a company. You should have the teams or systems with the right expertise in place beforehand.

- Identify which industries are growing faster than yours or have the potential to. That's the direction you want to go.

- Generate excitement. Promote the expansion internally to get employees on board and passionate about the changes first. This will engage customers later.

LESSON 4

VOLUNTEER

You've got to find a way to make people know you're there.
—Nikki Giovanni

The reasons to go above and beyond the assigned duties you're paid to do are many.

Sometimes that reason is, simply, you're new, it's your first day or week on the job, and you're trying to make a fine impression. Or maybe you're vying for a promotion and trying to catch the boss's eye. Maybe you're just bored and want to learn more.

Whatever the impetus, know that volunteering can alter the course of your career.

Just be mindful that some tasks are more like office housework than others. While everyone should certainly pitch in to clean the shared fridge, what's more advantageous to your career is to focus on missions that add value without being so hidden from sight.

Maybe that means volunteering for work that connects you to an influential person, puts you face-to-face with different departments, or helps you develop new or existing skills.

Start with thinking like a team player and seeing the bigger picture. Seek ways you can make a real impact by improving the flow of your company. Ask your coworkers and people in other departments for ideas on what would make their workday lives easier.

For me, volunteering started mostly with boredom and curiosity, but showing initiative and anticipating needs proved to be fine lessons once again.

Entry-Level Work

Having lost my business, I thought maybe I should attend junior college and see how that would go. I enrolled in classes for the semester starting the end of September 1972 at LA Valley City College. My four classes were spread out over an eight-hour period with long intervals between classes.

College didn't go well for me. I was bored and not very engaged. So, within a couple of months, I dropped two of the classes. By the time the first semester finished, I knew attending college was not for me.

I had completely oriented myself to spending as many weekends as possible skiing with my friends, and I quickly ran out of money.

In early 1973, I was looking for work *and* planning my next ski season. My goal? To make enough money to buy a new pair of skis and boots along with gas, lodging, and lift tickets to be ready for the winter ski season.

I thought an entry-level shipping clerk job was appropriate based on my experience at Alexander's, and time spent filling out UPS and US Postal Service shipping forms.

I began my search by sifting through the classifieds in the daily newspapers and found two companies in Glendale looking for shipping clerks. One was Levitz Furniture, a well-known furniture retailer with a large warehouse and show-room. The other was SEMCO, a division of Products Research & Chemical Corporation (PRC). I knew little about PRC other than that it manufactured goods.

Both interviews were on the same day. That morning, I dressed in clean jeans, a collared shirt, and tennis shoes. At six foot four inches and 160 pounds, I was tall and thin with long blond hair down to my shoulders.

At Levitz, my first interview, I remember being impressed by the modern warehouse, new forklifts, and material-handling equipment. It looked like a nice place to work.

When I arrived at SEMCO for my second interview, the lobby was full of other people waiting to be interviewed too. With a recession going on, getting a job was tough. More people were competing for fewer jobs than ever.

I waited for about an hour before being called into the interview room where I was introduced to Danny Iwamota, the shipping supervisor.

Danny got right to the interview. He set out his goals and expectations for the shipping clerk position.

This interview stood out for its clarity and straightforward set of questions. Among other topics, Danny questioned me on my experience filling out UPS, USPS, and common carrier shipping forms. He said he liked to keep the area clean and organized, and that he expected inventory in its proper place at the start and end of each shift. He also expected employees to clock in fifteen minutes early.

Danny made it clear the shipping and warehouse areas would be swept every day before the shift ended. He asked if I could drive a forklift. I replied, "Sure."

But I *didn't* tell him I had never driven one. I was sure I *could*. If he had directly asked me if I had ever driven a forklift before, I would have answered differently. I often wonder, if he had asked it this way, would I have gotten the job?

This tough interview was highly specific to the job at hand, which means I did not learn much about SEMCO's business itself.

Before long, I received offers from both Levitz and SEMCO. The Levitz offer had a slightly higher hourly wage than SEMCO, but Danny Iwamoto had impressed me.

When you're new and inexperienced, you want to work for someone who is willing to explain things, who has a precise vision with clear-cut expectations, and who knows how to

Choose People

It happens sometimes. You get two job offers at the same time, perhaps on the same day. Maybe one even pays a little more, but you find yourself still torn between the two. You might even be more tempted by the role with the slightly lower salary. So how do you decide?

For me, it comes down to the people. Maybe because that lesson from my dad sticks with me so well: Always find the best of the best to learn from.

So, ask yourself this: Did you meet someone in your interviews that you could see serving as a role model or a mentor? Someone you could see encouraging you or inspiring you down the road?

Philosophical self-help author Bob Proctor describes a mentor as "someone who sees more talent and ability within you than you see within yourself, and helps bring it out of you."

If you find that person as early as your interview, that's a good sign and a good starting point for deciding.

communicate. I felt that with Danny. He set the tone for me and made a good impression, so the decision was easy. I took the SEMCO offer.

I did not know it then, but this would be one of the most consequential, life-changing decisions I would ever make. My choice had been about the person, not the company, although, ironically, this was a job in a division of a company that I would eventually run someday.

At the time, I was just excited to know that, at $3.10 an hour, I could quickly save up to buy a new set of skis and boots. I'd be ready for ski season! And that had Mike's stamp of approval all over it.

On my first day at SEMCO, I was still a teenager turning twenty in a few months. I lived at home and wasn't concerned about my future beyond wanting to have money in my pocket and fun on the weekends.

What did I need to know to become a good entry-level shipping clerk? Well, I had to learn the clerical part first, which included picking orders, keeping track of inventory, preparing bills of lading for common carrier truck shipments, documenting the UPS and USPS books, and preparing air documentation for air freight shipments.

And I had to figure out how to drive a forklift.

We used forklifts to move and stack pallets of inventory in the warehouse racks as well as to load and unload trucks and move new inventory from the production area to the warehouse. I watched carefully as the two other shipping clerks used the forklift and asked questions about its operations.

Danny showed me how to remove and replace the natural gas tank and properly use the forks in different situations.

My chance to operate the forklift on my own came in the first month when they let me use it for certain simple tasks before my upcoming forklift driver's test. The simplest task was to use the forklift with a trash hopper attachment and drive to the various trash cans in the plant.

George Sergiattis, our maintenance guy, followed me and would lift and dump the trash into the hopper.

George had been born with a disability, and his left arm and leg were of limited use. Because he walked with a limp, to compensate for it, he had developed his right arm and leg, which were powerfully built up.

Even with his limitations, he was probably the strongest person in the company. He could easily heave the heavy trash cans into the hopper using one hand to grab the can and one leg to balance on. He could do this while constantly complaining about various things and people he defined as problems.

George was not impressed with my abilities to drive the forklift that day and made sure everyone within earshot heard about it. Forklift technology uses the rear wheel for steering, which is completely different than driving a car, so I got off to a rocky start, but each day I would do better.

Within a week, I had reached the point where I thought I was ready to get my license and make it through the employee probation period.

The next week, I took my test and passed. Off and running!

Going Above and Beyond

As I quickly mastered my daily tasks, I became bored with the work, so I sought other areas to help out and learn new duties. I knew that understanding the business better would help me develop relationships.

First, though, I decided to learn more about this plastic injection molding business called SEMCO.

I learned SEMCO designed and manufactured proprietary packaging for use with adhesives and sealants, trade named SEMKIT®. The SEMKIT® product line was a patented package designed to bundle two-part reactive adhesives and sealants until they were ready for use.

The user could mix and apply the adhesive or sealant directly from the SEMKIT® in the assembly of aircraft and automotive parts and other durable goods such as electronics and telecommunication products.

I learned that SEMCO was owned by Products Research & Chemical Corporation (PRC), a small NYSE-listed public company that developed and manufactured sealants and adhesives for the aerospace and defense, telecommunications, automotive, glass, and construction industries.

The company had evolved from a small distributor into a manufacturer with its own proprietary technology under the leadership of George Gregory, a Russian immigrant and chemist who joined PRC in 1948.

I also learned that the workflow at a small manufacturer like SEMCO was managed in a sequential way. A customer service person took an order over the phone, then passed it to a clerk who typed up the multipage order form. One page was removed from the rest and placed in an order file in customer service. The rest of the order was sent to the Planning Department. There, a work order was typed up, attached to the order, and sent to manufacturing or to the warehouse if it was in stock.

When the product was in stock, it was picked up by the shipping clerks and put on a pallet or packed for UPS or air freight. After documents were prepared, shipping arranged for delivery to the customer.

If the product needed to be manufactured first, the order went to manufacturing and later moved to shipping.

When the order shipped, the packing list would be added to the shipment. The order's final page went back to customer service so the order could be closed out and billed. This was a straightforward but totally manual process.

These days, a computer enterprise resource planning process is used to manage all this, but the underlying process is still the same.

The problems we had were almost always related to order status. It was difficult to know which part of the factory held the orders at any given time.

If someone wanted to get a status on an order for a customer, the only way to do it was to track down the paperwork. That meant calling or visiting each department and asking those responsible when they expected to complete their work and send the paperwork to the next department. Then we could estimate the time needed for any other steps in the process and provide that information to customer service.

To do this, the company had expediters find the status of an order and (if necessary) give it priority over other orders. That, then, created a new set of issues for getting the other orders out on time.

The expediters were always overworked. They managed the work by using the phone to talk to those in charge of the various planning, manufacturing, quality, shipping, and receiving departments to get the latest status on orders.

They would always call shipping first to see if the orders had made it through the other departments. If not, they would work backward through the process until they found the order.

If I received a call in shipping, the only action required was to look in the order file and see if the requested order was ready for shipment.

After a few of these calls, I asked the expediters if they wanted me to look for the order. After all, I went in and out of the production areas all day picking up finished inventory and moving it to shipping.

This was easy for me to do. I just stopped by each of the production departments and checked in the order file to see if the order was there. If not, I would search the others as I made my way through those areas.

Once I located the order, I would ask the area's supervisor when it would be completed. Then, once I returned to shipping, I would call the expediter and let him or her know the status. Doing this was interesting and fun, *and* it made my day go faster.

It also made a big impression on the expediters, who told customer service about it. They, in turn, told the general manager of SEMCO. I was getting serious recognition for being a team player.

While all this was positive for me, the downside was that my fellow shipping clerks believed I was doing more than them. That made them look bad.

Danny was not sure what to make of it. While he liked my initiative, he thought it was up to the expediters to do the work I was doing, but since I was getting all of my other work done, he decided to monitor the situation.

One of the other shipping clerks told me straight out that I was making him look bad and to concentrate only on the shipping role. This shocked me. I liked the other clerks and we got along well, but I kept doing the extra work and let them know they could do it, too.

I continued to help my new friends in customer service and their expediters. Besides, I liked getting noticed for the extra effort.

And wouldn't you know it, before long I was made lead shipping clerk.

The clerk who complained I was making him look bad? Well, he suddenly reported to me. And not surprisingly, he left the company shortly after.

The new pace and scope of our shipping area became a normal part of our work.

I had been validated in following my instincts, proving once again that it never hurts to ask how you can be of additional service to those around you.

LESSON 5

ADVOCATE FOR CUSTOMERS

Customer service shouldn't just be a department;
it should be the entire company.
—Tony Hsieh

The word *advocate* gets used often in business in regards to branding. Brand advocates have taken over the internet, and as a result, numerous articles online talk about customer advocacy as if it's something that loyal customers do to promote companies.

To add to the confusion, there's now also "advocacy marketing," which is a strategy used to get existing customers to share their positive experiences with other people. Advocacy marketing companies boast online that "marketing effectiveness is increased by 54% when advocacy is employed."

Companies from Tesla to Starbucks to Apple offer everything from cash discounts to gift cards and publicity to get customers to *advocate* their products or share photos online.

I would call that *brand* advocacy, though.

What I'm talking about here is a true customer advocate—someone *inside* the company who is rooting for the customers above all else.

According to Cambridge Dictionary, a customer advocate is "a person whose job is to find out the needs of a company's customers, and to make sure that the customers are provided with what they want."

To me, that sounds like the plain old watered-down customer-service language from textbooks decades ago. What I envision is something a notch above that.

To me, customer advocacy is both an art and a science. It's pleasing customers while showing empathy and patience, but it's also managing time and understanding cost-efficient ways to resolve problems. It's knowing when to put a customer's interests above the company's, when to refer a competitor's product over your own (to maintain good faith), and when to go straight to upper management.

Customer service advocates ask many questions so processes are clear and customers feel heard and valued. They say the customer's name and schedule follow-ups around the customer's preferred availability. They create procedures to ensure that problems don't repeat, and they recommend products and services that better match customers' needs.

Customer advocates also encourage feedback and understand the approval processes. They are the focal point for learning about and improving the customer experience—and if they're doing their job well, they keep the company honest and on its toes.

They're kind of like customer service agents on steroids, but not exactly.

Reading various marketing experts online, I see "customer advocacy" being called "a transitional movement making waves in sales and marketing organizations."

Funny enough, though, it's a title I gave to myself in the 1970s—way back when customer service was weighted down with rotary phones, typewriters, carbon-copy filing forms, and on-foot missions to find answers.

I had never heard the title before. And customer advocacy certainly wasn't a movement. It was just something born within me at that time—part intuitive, part altruistic, part self-driven.

Maybe I was just tired of being pestered by complaints I couldn't fix in a broken system.

My First Desk Job

In 1974, both my personal and professional life were changing. I had gotten married, and at the end of that year, SEMCO's general manager was promoted to general manager of PRC, the parent of SEMCO.

His first order of business? To offer me a customer service position in that part of the company.

Given the job I was doing, the new SEMCO general manager wasn't happy about my leaving. He agreed to the change but swore to get me back as soon as he could.

I reported to duty in customer service at PRC, my first desk job. I was excited to learn more about the products and customers.

PRC manufactured sealants, adhesives, and coatings for the aerospace, marine, insulated glass, and construction industries. These products were formulated by chemists who worked in a research and development lab in Burbank, California. The products were manufactured in large mixers in a batch process either in our main plant in Glendale or at a second plant in Gloucester City, New Jersey.

PRC made more than a thousand formulations, and many were tested to strict aerospace and defense industry specifications. The synthetic rubber-based products all had short shelf lives, so we had to "make them to order" instead of making them in advance and keeping them in stock for immediate shipment.

Thus, the order planning and fulfillment process was complex and difficult to manage.

PRC was known for its high-quality proprietary products—*and* its poor customer service.

The customer service area consisted of five customer service clerks and two typists, one of whom also worked the telex machine, short for "teleprinter exchange." The device operated like a typewriter that transmitted through a telephone line.

At the other end was a printer that printed out messages on a thin piece of tape. The messages were sent in a kind of shorthand to minimize their size and keep the cost of each message down. Through the telex machine, we received orders from Latin America, Europe, and Asia.

The customer service clerks took orders by phone, mail, or telex and wrote up the order information, special instructions, price, billing, and shipping terms. The orders were then typed onto an order form and sent to the Planning Department.

Planning personnel would determine if we had the raw materials on hand, then set up a production order. From there, the orders moved sequentially to all the departments responsible for production, quality control, and packaging. And then from there, they went to shipping to be readied for the customers.

Like at SEMCO, once the process began, keeping track of the orders was difficult. If a customer inquired about an order's status, providing the timely, accurate information was not easy.

In my new role, I was in the position of needing support from the expediters and others to find out the order status for our customers. Most of the people I called did provide information if they had it. From that, I could develop a picture of the overall status of the order.

But others around the company weren't interested in providing information, and the person who supervised the Planning Department was one of them. To him, our calls were secondary to his objective of planning orders for production. His attitude created much frustration for the customer service team.

When to Show Your Teeth

There was this guy, Bill Ottinger, who had gotten the nickname Wild Bill in our office for his big personality. He would always say, "You're gonna give me a better price, right?"

His was the account that always got passed down to the new guy. And I was the new guy.

Wild Bill was some thirty years older than me and worked at the General Services Administration (GSA), the government arm that purchased our products. He would call nearly every day with his small orders, whenever an air base needed a couple boxes of this or that sealant. He was a nice guy but persistent with his price haggling.

My job was to talk to customers, write down their orders correctly, and give them a price with the terms of sale. Each customer had a card with his or her purchasing history and any special notes or price discounts that applied.

There were no computer systems back in the day, so we had a price list and had to reference it to know volume discounts. These were numbers that higher-level marketing people decided on. I had no latitude to change those. But I did. Several times.

Wild Bill had a way of squeezing good prices out of you. For those first few orders, I would acquiesce and give him a 5 to 10% discount, markdowns that he did not earn or legitimately deserve as a small-order customer.

It bothered me, though, that he was making me do it against my will, so I started to get firmer in my pushback. I began to focus on the value of what we were supplying to him. Maybe I should be increasing the price?

I decided one day to tell him no. I drew a line in the sand and said, "I can't give you a volume-price discount on this." Nobody at the company had ever done that before with him. I made the decision spontaneously without consulting my boss first.

There was a lot of back-and-forth pushing in that awkward conversation before Bill finally said, "You do what you gotta do." The call ended with tension and, minutes later, he was on the phone with my boss giving him an earful: "What are you doing to that kid, feeding him raw meat?"

Ironically, Bill's third-party endorsement would haunt me for years—in a good way.

(continued on page 53)

My boss, fortunately, had known the guy forever and was able to smooth things over with him, but more importantly, he backed me up on what I had said. He did call me into his office because he wanted to hear my defense and let me know that I should have consulted him first, but he also told me, "You did the right thing."

And like that, I got respect from my boss. My pushback even changed the whole way we dealt with that customer from then on.

The story also got around the office and became a bit legendary. Soon, all my peers knew that even though I was a nice kid, I wasn't a chump, which was the reputation enhancer I needed at the time.

And perhaps most importantly, the situation validated my instincts and helped me trust myself when pushing back with tough customers. I grew an increased appreciation for the value of our services in the end.

As customer service clerks, we were always on the defensive when the limited information from planning and other departments turned out to be wrong. Our customers who followed up would loudly complain that they couldn't rely on the order status we provided.

The broken process would need someone with more authority than me to fix it, as I could not overcome the obstacles on my own.

What did I do? I approached the problem differently so I could at least provide *my* customers with better information and do it *before* they called me to follow up on their orders.

My goal was to never have customers call back after they made their first order inquiry.

So, I set up a simple process. If a customer called to follow up on an order, I got the best status I could and provided it.

Then I set up a thirty-one-day file and would put a copy of the order in that file for my follow-up three days before the new ship date. For instance, if the order had to ship on the tenth of the month, I would file it for follow-up on the seventh of the month.

When the seventh came, I would pull the order and track it down to see if it would be ready to ship on the tenth and if not, why not?

Then I would call the customer before the tenth and let the person know either that the order was shipping (the good news) or was not shipping and why (the bad news).

Either way, our customers were grateful that I had called. And for those whose orders were on time, they gained confidence that someone was looking after them.

Many times I heard them say they were disappointed about the order status but appreciated knowing so they could let *their* team know.

This worked well and made the job much easier for me. If we missed the ship date multiple times, customers would complain to our management, but most of the time, they went out of their way to say they appreciated my efforts to communicate. It also helped that, when a manager came down to find out what was going on with the order, I could provide detail on why it was late and where it was in the process.

This became a simple solution for me, but it did not address the root causes of our dysfunctional production system. I would get to that problem later.

Becoming a Boss

Reports of what I was doing impressed managers throughout the company. At the end of 1976, I was offered a promotion to go back to SEMCO as the customer service supervisor. I accepted.

Mostly, I was glad to get out of a frustrating and negative environment created by a complex product line and a dysfunctional sales and operations process at PRC.

This new role at SEMCO marked the first time a team reported directly to me. Supervising the customer service group of five employees offered me the chance to develop as a leader.

By this time, I had been with the company for three years. We now had a little boy named Michael, named after my brother, born in 1975; he would be followed by our son Joshua Scot in 1978, whose middle name, Scot, came from my brother's middle name. It was important to me that my brother be remembered.

As you can imagine, the promotion and pay increase came at a good time. I was excited to move up in the company.

...

Back at SEMCO, I worked with distributors who stocked and sold our products to small- and midsized customers as well as large customers including Northrop, Lockheed, Boeing, and GE, who ordered directly from us.

My team took orders over the phone while dealing with all the day-to-day clerical activities. This gave me time to focus on new initiatives and resolve customer service problems.

We still did not have a computer-based integrated enterprise management information system to manage demand and production. That would come years later. But we did manage our financials on a computer system, so we had reports on customer sales, margins, accounts receivable and payable, and so on.

The Art of the Power Walk

The corporate power walk has become so popular over recent decades, it now has its own acronym: MBWA, also known as Management by Walking Around. It's a strategy that gets big props in the book by Karin Hurt and David Dye called *Winning Well: A Manager's Guide to Getting Results—Without Losing Your Soul*, but it's also one that I've been intuitively doing on my own since the mid-1970s.

The expression refers, quite obviously, to the practice of managers who saunter in a random, unplanned way throughout their company's offices and factories to chat with employees and observe firsthand the undertakings in each department.

When done properly, MBWA is a powerful way to build trust when managers take the time to truly connect with employees and customers. That is, they don't simply make an appearance or dive right into work and numbers. A manager needs to linger and build relationships; talk about habits and needs; not point out negative observations without acknowledging what's going right; pass on some insights about what they saw working well in another department or location to create a sort of organic corporate cross-pollination of information.

I do it differently today than I did almost fifty years ago, since these days I have seventy-two factories around the world. But I still go to each when I can and walk around and talk to the people. It's fun and probably the most important part of my job. For me to perform well, I need a connection with the people doing the actual work so I can understand their needs.

Just recently in November, at a factory that wasn't doing well, where quality had deteriorated over the past year and where PowerPoint presentations had provided little insight, I took to the floor to talk to workers and, sure enough, they precisely knew the problem.

In forty minutes I learned from every angle what had caused the breakdown. A new program requiring statistical analysis had become so time consuming that operator training had stopped and the typical debriefings between shifts had ended. I walked away knowing where to start in addressing the disconnects.

So, call it a curiosity tour or MBWA, but the mere act of listening face-to-face to the people who roll up their sleeves every day and deal with customers or manufacturing or any hands-on service is, I believe, the best practice a manager can do.

Unfortunately, we still had to either call or walk to the Production Department to find the status of orders. This became my daily habit throughout the rest of my career. I'd "power walk" all over the place, knowing what I wanted to accomplish during these walks.

Over time, my walk through the departments made me stand out compared to other employees and managers. I think it also amused some people more than it impressed them, but doing a power walk suited me well. I got things done quickly and could sort out many problems.

As a result, I began expanding the role of customer *service* to that of customer *advocate*. This created a new dynamic as someone who would challenge the status quo.

One simple construct has informed my decision-making ever since: The customer comes first, so systems and processes need to be designed to satisfy customer needs above all else.

Some forty-five years later, that concept is becoming a movement.

LESSON 6

NEVER STOP LEARNING

*Education is what people do to you
and learning is what you do for yourself.*
—Joichi Ito

You've probably heard the one about the definition of insanity being "doing the same thing over and over and expecting different results." Whether these words were uttered from the mouth of Albert Einstein or not is debatable, but the underlying point isn't.

It's similar to that other unattributable quote: "Old ways won't open new doors," and these clichés are out there for a reason. Life and problems never stop coming, and they're shapeshifters, presenting themselves in new guises all the time. So to stay ahead of them, we need to arm ourselves with enough information to navigate this world skillfully.

That's why I never stop learning. I'm like Warren Buffett in that way. I read most of the time.

It's been said that the person who adapts best along the way wins in the end, so I try to stay a couple steps ahead of the game if I can.

The immediate rewards are in personal development, such as a sense of purpose, serenity, and satisfaction with oneself. Research has even shown that the more ambitious our goals are, the happier we are.

Learning has also been linked to health and longevity. Being engrossed in a stimulating activity or in understanding new material helps us blossom with age and may delay signs of dementia and Alzheimer's disease by exercising the brain's neural connections and stimulating new ones.

So, take it upon yourself, at whatever age you are now, to commit to learning something new every day for the rest of your life and to witness how it changes you. The endeavor might stimulate more curiosity. It might make you irreplaceable at work. Your new interest might attract new friends, bring you into a new career, or align you with your passion. Or it might even bring you out of a funk.

Every interaction is a chance to learn something from someone else. Keep seeking ways to improve yourself and to learn from others. You'll probably find that people like you a lot more, too, when you're trying to learn from them.

Try to make it a habit to set aside time every evening to read new books, follow podcasts, update yourself with the news, or practice a hobby you've always wanted to learn. Turn off your phone, the TV, or any devices that distract you from your goal.

When you have a broader array of interests and knowledge, you're better able to connect with a wider variety of people on a more profound level, which opens you up to opportunities and collaborations that could further your career and life goals. At least that's how it has always been for me.

Spreading Advocacy

Making the change to *advocate* meant working with my team to quickly follow up on any customer issue with the respective departments involved. If customers had a quality issue, we would address that. If they had a problem with a credit memo, we would sort it out. If a price or discount was in question, we would get it straightened out. (You get the picture.)

Before this, customer service reps were focused on fielding questions on issues and then giving them to someone else to follow up. This practice created quite a variety in the level of customer service, depending on the responsiveness of people in various departments.

But this new advocacy approach became a big hit with our customers and especially with our distributors. Before that, they felt like second-class citizens.

I also needed to create a positive relationship with everyone I had to work with to solve customer service problems.

I was at the center, both doing the leg work (literally) and taking the heat from customers. I made it a part of my style to always communicate the situation and ask for help in resolving it. Fortunately, I could count on most team members to assist.

The benefit of this approach for me was that senior managers in sales, manufacturing, quality, and engineering took an interest in mentoring me. They willingly answered my questions; thus, I was learning the business from many perspectives.

I applied that learning to my day-to-day work and soon got promoted to manager of sales administration, reporting to the national sales manager. That position gave me more responsibility for pricing and distributor policy.

At the same time, I was encouraged to continue developing relationships with our network of distributors.

Baptism by Fire

My new boss, Skip Moline, was a legend in our industry. An old-school salesman, he spent as much time in restaurants and bars as in the office, and he also traveled and met with customers.

When he was in town, the day went mostly like this: In the morning, he would be in the office until about noon and then go to lunch with one of our salespeople. They would meet customers at one of the restaurants or bars the company had an account with. Mainly, they met purchasing agents and engineers working in Southern California's aerospace industry.

During a typical week, they would lunch with a Lockheed rep at Sardo's restaurant in North Hollywood. Another day, they would lunch at the Bat Rack in Santa Monica, where they met with a Northrop or Rockwell rep. Another day at a restaurant in Long Beach, they would meet with Douglas Aircraft people.

These lunches would run late into the day. This was an alcohol-fueled Mad Men sort of practice that, in the 1970s, was considered a normal way of doing business. I was left on my own in the office most afternoons to run the rest of the business.

During those afternoons, I would be faced with customer questions such as, what was our latest price or terms on a quote, or authorization requests for a product return, or permission to ship less than a minimum order. All these policy questions were above my authority.

At first, I called around to the restaurant or bar where Skip was to get his advice or approval about the matter I was dealing with. But after a while, this became tedious and inefficient. Besides, often when I got ahold of him, he was not in a good frame of mind to make decisions anyway.

So, naturally, I began to make decisions on my own and to brief Skip the next morning. He would either agree and say "good job" or disagree and tell me what I had done wrong. Then he explained how I should think about an issue the next time it came up.

This trial-and-error mentoring process worked well for both Skip and me, as it accelerated my development and understanding of the business.

Highlights of a Good Sales Pitch

It's a myth that the best sales reps are born that way. Selling is a teachable skill anyone can learn. I am proof of that.

The approach I use as a business-to-business (B2B) operator is a little different than traditional selling. I create new products for partners, so I'm schooled in needs-satisfaction sales, but the underlying approach is similar to what makes any sales call fruitful.

Here are some key takeaways I've learned and some interesting numbers that back it up:

Understand all capabilities of your business. From the inside out, know what your company is capable of creating for that customer. Know what makes your company or product different. You should also have in your head one sentence that sums up what your company does, how they do it, and for whom.

Probe to understand. Top sales performers ask ten to fourteen questions per call on average, while the typical rep only asks about six*, so be sure to ask many broad, open-ended questions to keep the conversation going, such as: How can we help you improve your productivity? Spread your questions naturally throughout the conversation, listen carefully, and try to match your company's abilities with a need they have.

Listen more than talk. Research has shown that talking about your own company for more than two minutes kills the sale, and the more speaker switches per minute, the higher your chances of a second meeting. Top sales reps talk *at most* for 46% of a sales call. That means the best sales reps listen for at least 54%.*

Acknowledge your competition early. When you do mention the competitor early on in your sales call, your chances of closing a deal go up by 49%.*

Don't discuss pricing in the first third of your pitch. Top-performing reps talk about pricing on average thirty-eight to forty-six minutes into an hour-long sales call. Talking money in the first fifteen minutes usually breaks the deal.*

(continued on page 65)

Focus on the value of your product or service. Don't tell buyers how something works; explain the results they will get. Offer up customer testimonials and statistics when appropriate.

Ask for the sale. Don't forget to close the deal. Share a focused, actionable solution that your company or product can offer, leave time to discuss next steps, and always follow up!

*Research from Gong, an intelligence platform that has studied over a million B2B sales-call recordings

Skip also wanted to develop me as a potential outside salesperson. He put together a list of targets for me to cold call, then gave me some product training and product sales brochures. I would do sales one day a week and report on my progress.

I turned out to be terrible at selling. Mostly, I could not get past the receptionist desk when making cold calls. When I did, my pitch was so bad, I never made a sale.

Knowing I was unhappy in this role, Skip called off this experiment after a few months. I was relieved. At the same time, I admired those on our sales team. As rainmakers, they were bringing in new opportunities and closing deals.

I knew that if I were to progress in the company, I would need to figure out what their secrets were.

In the meantime, my customer advocate strategy was improving our relationships with distributors, but a black cloud was on the horizon that our management didn't respond to.

For close to two decades, the company's main product, the SEMKIT®, had been protected by a patent. This had become our largest and most profitable product line, representing close to 50% of our sales. But before long, its patent would run out.

We had increased prices regularly on this product line because of our patent position, but the company had not re-invested at the level we should have to stay viable. Quality and service were suffering.

More than that, the injection molding machines and molds used to make the SEMKIT® were aging and needed regular maintenance. This caused cost, quality, and production issues that affected on-time delivery and increased customer complaints—a problem that had festered for years.

More alarming, we found out that several of our distributors were planning to band together and invest in their own molds. When the patent expired, they would make a knockoff product and cut out SEMCO altogether.

PRC Chairman and CEO George Gregory and PRC President Dean Willard decided it was time for a management change.

They hired Dick Cude as the new corporate vice president and general manager of SEMCO.

Over the years, Dick would go on to become an important mentor to me. From him, I would learn an enormous amount on how to be an effective leader.

Dick Cude was a dynamic leader who had held senior executive positions at several manufacturing companies, including one he founded and later sold to Ren Plastics.

When Dick introduced himself to me, he said he had heard a lot about me and looked forward to working with me. He wanted to develop me so I'd be worth more than the company could pay me.

I did not understand what he meant then. In time, though, I understood it to mean that every worker needed to create more value than the wages the company paid. For those in management, the value should be *multiples* higher, especially as that person rises to top levels.

I worked closely with Dick to identify areas that needed improvement at SEMCO. We set out making fundamental changes to our business processes and improved the performance and profitability of the division.

When we talked about my failed experiment in sales, he said the company was sending the sales teams to a sales training course. Did I want to go? Yes. It was an opportunity to travel to Chicago and meet new members of the team, but at the same time, I was not sure the training would help.

I did not realize it then, but it would become one of the most important courses I would ever take.

The sales training put on by Xerox Corporation was a combination of classroom training and role playing. The Xerox approach centered on what the trainers called "need/satisfaction" selling based on listening and not talking. That concept appealed to me.

The idea was to get in front of a customer and give a broad overview of the company's capabilities, then ask probing questions to learn the customer's challenges in using adhesives and sealants. The objective was to listen to their answers and then match a product or service that could address their challenges.

This way of selling turned on a light for me. It marked the beginning of a solution sales approach that I've used ever since.

•••

Although we were making good progress improving the business, we still had to repair our relationships with our distributors and get them back on our side.

Dick offered me a new position of national account manager with responsibility for our large direct accounts and our distributors. With newfound confidence from my sales training, I felt like I was ready to make the move and quickly accepted.

Imagine! In a little more than five years, I had risen from shipping clerk to national accounts manager and part of Dick's executive team.

The lesson I had learned at Alexander Auto Headlining—always anticipate what needs to be done and do it before people ask—had served me well.

I knew, though, it would take more than that to keep progressing. At twenty-six years old, I was completely focused on learning the business and continuing to grow.

LESSON 7

BUILD TRUST

*If people like you, they will listen to you,
but if they trust you, they'll do business with you.*
—Zig Ziglar

The importance of trust is summed up nicely in this quote from social media influencer Dhar Mann: "Trust takes years to build, seconds to break, and forever to repair." It's like crumpling up a perfect piece of paper, he says. "You can smooth it over, but it's never going to be the same again."

Trust is crucial in sustaining productive relationships. When people don't trust, they avoid each other, play games, and undermine one another's efforts. It's a recipe for a toxic relationship.

Stephen M. R. Covey, author of *The Speed of Trust*, makes the argument that trust, in the commercial setting, affects two outcomes: speed and cost.

Whether driven by unethical behavior or incompetence, low trust causes friction, he says, citing that when trust goes down, speed also goes down, but costs go up. Inversely, when trust goes up, speed goes up and costs go down.

Covey points out that lack of trust creates hidden agendas, interpersonal conflict, office politics, interdepartmental rivalries, win-lose thinking, defensive posturing, and overly protective communication, all of which slow down progress in the workplace as we become suspicious about other people's motivations, integrity, and their very ability to produce results.

On the other hand, trust, he says, builds loyalty, creates a winning culture, and encourages customers to purchase more and to refer more people, products, and services. It elevates thinking to the big-picture level and accelerates decision-making.

When I first entered management, I was only twenty-five. Everyone was much older and more experienced than me, so I had a lot of pressure to prove myself in those new relationships, especially with the distributors who had already heard too many promises that hadn't been kept.

What I learned was that broken relationships can be mended with patience and perseverance. Don't expect too much too soon, and do celebrate small milestones in reconnecting as they happen.

Establishing My Reputation

Dick and I agreed I would organize a trip to visit our network of distributors. Other than my recent training in Chicago, I had never been on a business trip before. I talked to all the distributors on the phone but had not met them in person.

My objective was to sit down with all the distributors and find out what they thought we could do to improve our relations, products, quality, and service. I'd ask probing questions and listen to the responses, develop a list of concerns, and commit to addressing the concerns within a defined period.

However, this plan fell apart rapidly with my first visit to an unhappy distributor. That started it. I was under fire for the rest of the week. I knew that how I responded to them and followed through would determine if my reputation as a problem solver would continue to grow—or if I would crash and burn.

The business trip began well enough as I arrived for my first visit at the John W. Blair company in Westerville, Ohio. Owner John Blair was one of the leaders in the movement to invest in molds, set up a distributor consortium, and have the group make a knockoff of the SEMKIT® product.

I first met with Dave Morris, Blair's general manager, whom I got along with well. We spent the day touring the Blair operations and discussing customer service and quality problems.

In addition to stocking and selling our products, our distributors also had repackaging lines, where they would fill our (and other manufacturers') adhesives and sealants into small packages, including our SEMKITs. This lucrative business created a local service process that their customers valued.

I learned about many ways we could improve in order to better address how John and Dave managed this process.

That evening, we met with John and his wife at his house for drinks and then on to his club for dinner.

John was known to have a difficult personality. He had started his business as a manufacturer's representative and built it into a successful regional adhesive and sealant distributor and contract packager.

But my probing-question approach did not fly with him. He frequently stopped me from asking questions with questions of his own, and he challenged everything I said.

He was an experienced operator; I still looked like a teenager. The whole evening ended up being a rocky one.

John's opening question was, "What are you going to do about your terrible service?" Then he followed with questions like, "What makes you think *you* can fix things? I have had *vice presidents* from your company make me promises that they never kept."

And more: "I don't need you guys. We will make our own products; you guys compete with me; why should I believe anything you say?"

And more yet: "I find out you are selling direct to my customers, and your sales manager lies to me about it."

On it went like this through drinks and dinner.

After dinner, we went to the bar for a nightcap. By then, we all had consumed quite a few drinks, and I'd had enough. The more John drank, the meaner he got. I tried again to explain how we would respond to his complaints, but I made no progress.

I finally stopped him and said, "Look, I know you don't believe me, but give me that napkin." Then I took the napkin and wrote out a list of complaints I would work on to resolve. I said I would come back in three months for another meeting.

Then I signed it and told him, "If I don't get these things done by the time I come back, you can call me anything you want and do anything you want. But I'm done tonight."

This took him aback a bit—at first. Then he laughed and said, "Fair enough."

Thankfully, the rest of the night went fine. By pushing back while taking responsibility and making a concrete commitment, I bought time.

And I showed him that, even being young, he could not push me around.

Our Terrible Service

That week, I visited four more distributors. While the first was the toughest, the others had similar complaints. A few weeks later, I visited the rest of the US distributors, where I heard more of the same complaints.

This gave me a clear understanding of the issues we needed to resolve to benefit everyone and, ultimately, to get the distributors to back down from forming a consortium to make SEMKITs themselves.

The six dominant issues were:

1. Our sales policies were too restrictive. "Can't we mix products to fill up a truck shipment instead of having to take a full truckload of one product?"

2. We were too slow to resolve quality problems. "My customer knows the product is out of specification. Why do we have to wait so long for a replacement?"

3. Many times, we quoted lower prices to their customers than they did. "We have been working on that customer for six months. When he asked for a quote, we used

your published prices and then found out you quoted them *directly* with your lower wholesale prices."

4. We were slow to provide quotes for orders. "I could have closed a sale, but because it took so long for you to provide pricing, I lost the order."

5. We would promise to resolve billing problems and not follow through. "For example, you quoted us a special price and billed us at a higher price. Yet no one was taking responsibility for resolving the discrepancy."

6. We would raise prices without enough notification. "You raise prices, and we get squeezed."

With Dick's support, I worked on resolving these issues. More times than not, the problems led back to Skip. He was a great salesman but not good on follow-up. He spent his time entertaining customers, and that was becoming a problem.

Dick, who had been sober for more than twenty years, kept a framed copy of the serenity prayer in his office: "God grant me the serenity to accept the things I cannot change, the courage to change the things I can, and the wisdom to know the difference."[1]

---

1 Reinhold Niebuhr *(1892–1971)*. Niebuhr used various versions of the prayer widely in sermons as early as 1934. The prayer spread rapidly, often without attribution to Niebuhr, through church groups in the 1930s and 1940s and was adopted and popularized by Alcoholics Anonymous and other twelve-step programs. The Serenity Prayer appeared in a sermon of Niebuhr's as part of the 1944 *A Book of Prayers and Services for the Armed Forces*, while Niebuhr himself first published it in 1951 in a magazine column. https://www.beliefnet.com/inspiration/galleries/who-wrote-the-serenity-prayer.aspx.

•••

By the late 1970s, the three-martini lunch as an accepted business practice was ending. But Skip had yet to accept this and the need to change. So, Dick entered into discussions with Skip about his future.

I was working on a set of policies and processes that addressed the issues raised by the distributors. By executing these, we would hopefully put an end to their threats of forming their own consortium to make SEMKITs.

We also set up a quick response system to be managed by the customer service team that reported to me. The goal was to respond to any distributor issue within two days. We worked to get that commitment from other managers, too.

We developed a commitment promise to our distributors that we could track and report our progress on a quarterly basis, and then formally communicated our plan to the distributors.

With that legwork done, we got to work improving our processes. Top of that list was cleaning up and organizing price lists and our pricing policy.

It had come to the CFO's attention that the margins of profit on our products were all over the place. There were two phenomena going on at SEMCO at the time. We were both undercharging and overcharging customers by treating similar customers very differently, favoring some over others. There wasn't a lot of discipline around pricing or a consistent way of handling that, and the price points for the same products varied greatly, mostly for the volume discounts.

The CFO was concerned that our profit margins were eroding and took a strong stand around that, holding the management accountable till adjusted.

This task was one that none of the senior level people wanted to tackle, so they gave it to me.

I welcomed the role as another mentoring opportunity and, simply, a chance to learn. I had continued to struggle with a little insecurity around being so young in management and not having a college degree. I figured this was something I probably should have learned in school, so I might as well dive in now and get to understanding these price lists.

The goal, for competitive reasons, was to determine whether we were over- or underpricing our products in general to ensure we were getting the right value in the marketplace.

I ended up redoing all the price lists to create clarity and relevance, especially clarifying economically the prices we set for larger volumes.

Researching all the pricing was grinder work, not fun at all, but it got me involved in cost accounting, and all that I learned helped to broaden my view as a business leader.

In the end, my efforts had a positive impact on our company's profitability, and because I was key in resolving that issue, I gained respect among my peers and bosses.

Assessing My Potential

So here I was, a kid off the streets, so to speak, with no college education, in his mid-twenties, and within five years I had already been given an important management opportunity.

My advancement sparked some discussions from above, such as, "What do we have here? How far can this kid punch above his weight?"

I was likeable, demonstrated potential and initiative, and was getting things done, so my name naturally caught the attention of PRC's president Dean Willard.

He wanted to know if, given the chance, could I offer something more? Could I critically self-assess and find my own blind spots? These were two crucial skills for anyone wanting to be considered for a bigger role in the organization. He also wanted to better understand my strengths and weaknesses, my quality of character, and my ability to change and adapt.

For these reasons, Dick approached me to say Dean wanted me to be assessed by an industrial psychologist. In the previous two years, the company had asked key executives and salespeople to go through this process to find out their capabilities and identify areas to develop through additional training.

I was kind of young for this type of expensive assessment, especially given that it was still a relatively new exploratory tool used rarely by our company at the time, so I felt honored to be given the attention. I was happy to go, and I appreciated that Dean was sponsoring this request.

So, I made an appointment with Dr. Bender, whose office was in Palos Verdes, California, overlooking the Pacific Ocean. In this full-day meeting, we first went through standard assessments such as the Rorschach test and other cognitive and intelligence testing.

For the second half of the day, we sat in his study in two comfortable chairs. He asked questions about my background, family, education, experience, ambitions, motivation, goals, and some basic business questions. For instance, he asked me to define EBIT. At that point, I had no idea what EBIT meant—earnings before interest and tax—and I didn't do well on his other finance-related questions either.

About a month later, Dr. Bender sent a report to Dean, Dick, and me that showed positive findings on my general intelligence and overall potential.

But his report suggested I did not have a broad perspective of business and politics and, likewise, my financial sophistication was limited. I needed to develop in these areas to be considered for higher levels of executive management.

Dr. Bender recommended I spend time reading about business, global politics, and other areas that would broaden my perspective. He also said I would benefit from basic finance and accounting training.

After I reviewed the report, I met with Dr. Bender again. While I was initially disappointed with the review, he gave me good ideas on how to expand my horizons, suggesting I read *Time, Newsweek, Business Week,* and *The Wall Street Journal.* He also gave me a list of business and history books and encouraged me to take courses on finance and accounting.

Until then, I had not been exposed to much financial information other than sales and gross margins reports, which were easy to understand. And although I saw our quarterly and annual reports, I didn't understand them.

This idea of purposefully aiming to broaden my perspective would become a lifelong habit for me. It helped me improve my judgments and decision-making as I continued to grow and develop.

The Value of Psychological Assessments

The cost of hiring a bad CEO—once you take into account severance, lost productivity, and missed opportunities—can go upward of $50 million for large-cap companies, according to an analysis by New York HR consultant Nat Stoddard.

Even small companies can't afford it, says Dr. Bradford Smart, author of *Topgrading: The Proven Hiring and Promoting Method That Turbocharges Company Performance*. He puts the cost of mishiring a CEO, for any company, between five and twenty-seven times the actual salary.

Either way, that's a costly mistake, so most organizations understandably preevaluate potential CEO candidates. In fact, nearly 75% of the 500+ companies polled in a Boston study by the Aberdeen Group reported using psychological assessments in their hiring process, from employee screening to managerial selection.

Employers want to know, will this person conflict with others at work? How smart is he or she? Do they have creative abilities? Do any behavioral tendencies exist that might impede managerial skills?

The process can be a bit intimidating, as no stone is left unturned. All your failures and successes are brought out into the open. Relationships with peers, subordinators, and supervisors are scrutinized. You are asked questions about substance use and abuse. Evaluations usually include intelligence tests, multiple personality questionnaires, and many hours of one-on-one clinical interviews with a psychologist.

But what an incredible opportunity to receive the most invaluable objective feedback you'll probably ever get about yourself in this life. So, if your company ever offers to psychologically evaluate you for a promotion, don't get paranoid and take it the wrong way. It's a chance to grow and learn about yourself, at no cost to you.

Today, so much more than thirty or forty years ago, there are CEO and senior executive coaches that help executives work through their weaknesses, and companies even tailor plans for helping potential managers develop.

If ever asked, I highly recommend you say yes to the opportunity.

Solving Problems

While I worked on Dr. Bender's suggestions, I continued to focus on getting things done. After all, it was close to three months since I'd had my first visit with John Blair. The time had come for me to meet with him again and get his feedback on the improvements we had committed to make.

I had plans to meet Dave Morris from Blair at a trade show and industry conference in Cleveland, so I suggested we visit John after that.

When I got to Cleveland, Dave told me that John was flying to the city in a private plane to have lunch with us. I asked Dave why he was making this effort, but Dave was vague about the reasons, which made me feel concerned.

The three of us met at a nice restaurant overlooking Lake Erie. After initial pleasantries, I asked John how he felt about the progress our company was making.

He replied by telling me that if we weren't making progress, he would not have flown up to see me!

John said he appreciated our efforts to address the issues, and if we continued to do this consistently, it would go a long way to rebuild trust.

"Have you been in touch with the other distributors?" I asked John.

He affirmed that they were all seeing progress and feeling better about our company's commitment to them.

I had also been in touch with these distributors myself and had heard good reviews directly from them, but I can't deny that hearing it from John himself was even sweeter.

The talk of setting up a consortium had eased and never again arose as a serious threat.

And that's how you build trust. By doing what you promise.

LESSON 8

LEARN TO SELL

*The questions you ask are more important
than the things you could ever say.*
—Thomas Freese

One in every nine American workers works in sales. The other eight? They work in sales too, says Daniel Pink, author of *To Sell Is Human: The Surprising Truth About Moving Others*. He calls it "non sales selling"—the everyday things we say and do to persuade others. It's a reality that doesn't settle well with many people, especially introverts, as the idea of sales conjures up images of pushy, spineless used car salesmen in checkered suits.

As Pink points out, however, times have changed. The information age has shifted the balance of power. Whereas sellers used to hold all the cards, making consumers feel vulnerable, potential buyers now have essentially the same amount of information, which, Pink explains, has taken much of the dishonesty out of traditional sales.

Networking, teamwork, asking for letters of recommendation, participating in meetings, and performance reviews are just a few of the ways in which we use our innate selling skills.

And selling is not only for the white-collar workers, either. The cashiers, Uber drivers, and fry cooks—anyone who speaks with customers or deals with managers and coworkers or who has ever had a job interview or asked for time off—are salespeople as well.

We're all trying to move and influence others on a daily basis to make people like us or see things from our point of view.

So, like it or not, we're salesmen.

The good news is, simply understanding this concept is an important revelation, says Dr. Cindy McGovern, author of *Every Job Is a Sales Job: How to Use the Art of Selling to Win at Work*, because once we embrace our inner salesperson, we can finally start to sharpen those skills.

Non-Sales Selling

Influencing others is an art form we can all learn. Below are a few persuasion tips suggested by Daniel Pink and Dr. Cindy McGovern:

- Plan a clear path for getting what you want.

- Be passionate about getting it.

- Be sensitive to how people are thinking about things.

- Subtly reflect back people's posture, inflection, and word choices to align with their perspective.

- Establish trust with those who can help you.

- Ask questions: it can be more effective than making statements.

- Learn to identify subtle opportunities that can lead to success.

- Move beyond the fear of rejection; learn how to promote yourself or ideas.

- Uncover hidden problems now, which can be more persuasive than problem-solving existing problems.

- Find the courage to ask for referrals, references, and introductions.

- Be mindful about how you explain your failures and rejections.

- Follow up on your requests, show gratitude, and always pay it forward.

- Stay in touch, even if the answer is a rejection.

Dr. McGovern, who used to sell "all day long" when she was a college professor, goes on to argue that we should be selling all the time even if in some unofficial way.

She's a proponent that we all have the tools we need to be successful at sales and that we've had them our whole lives. And I agree.

There are "selling opportunities" around us all the time,

and, as Dr. McGovern says, once we *realize* that we're selling, doors begin to open from every direction. We begin to impress bosses and appear more valuable to clients.

Even if you don't have the natural gift of gab, you should try to enjoy the idea of selling. Because you're doing it anyway, and if you're doing it poorly, things probably aren't going well in your life. So you might as well try.

"Trying is winning in the moment," as Dan Waldschmidt, an international businessman and author, likes to say. The worst people can say is no. Even then, the door isn't exactly shut if you know what you're doing.

I take the approach of Brian Tracy, another motivational speaker and author. I "treat objections as requests for further information." It has always served me well.

In this lesson, I found myself at a moment in my life where I was surrounded by salespeople. Learning about sales helped me not only grow the business but grow myself as a person. It's a skill I'm grateful to have learned.

Reaping the Rewards of Trust

For the next two years, we continued to improve our relations with these distributors, and our sales returned and grew. We had set clear policies to identify which customers we would sell to directly. We defined more specifically which territories and customers the distributors would support and how our company could help them develop new business. By building trust, they became more comfortable working with our sales team to do joint calls, finding and closing more sales as a result.

We also organized annual distributor meetings and allowed our distributors to air any issues they had in a transparent manner. Our senior management team attended the meetings as a way to show our commitment and hear their thoughts firsthand.

Our senior managers realized that I enjoyed the support of the distributors, and they trusted me to be transparent. This helped us develop a cooperative and positive energy for growth.

I loved this job and had a great time traveling around the country calling on customers as I continued to learn our business. I was earning a good salary and bonus based on results, and I even had my first company car.

I felt like I was adding value to the company more than what I was being paid. Thankfully, the managers kept giving me opportunities to continue learning and growing.

Driving Growth

By 1980, Skip had clearly neared the end of his time at the company. He had been warned about his performance and the need to change, but he wasn't able to change his old-school ways. Dick felt he had no alternative but to let him go.

Skip had been a strong mentor to me and always supportive, so I felt bad about his leaving.

After Dick let Skip go, he invited me into his office and walked me through his reasoning for making this change. Then he offered me the national sales manager job in addition to my current responsibilities.

Although I agreed, I was definitely concerned about one detail. I was only twenty-seven years old, and all five of the regional sales managers were over fifty. Two were World War II veterans. And all of them had much more sales experience than I did.

Return of the Three Martini Lunch

You'd have to have been there to believe it, but the '70s really were run by the Don Drapers of the world. There was a lot of socializing at the end of the day with smoke-filled rooms and small bars in many executives' offices.

At Christmastime, executives would roll in cases and cases of Scotch, keep them in the big closet, and then load them up in the trunks of our sales team's company cars for delivery to customers.

And the culture of the time went even beyond the casual office environment and the three martini lunches. Another expense was for business entertainment, such as tickets to concerts, baseball games, and golf outings, as well as hospitality rooms at conventions. This practice had become part of the business culture in the '70s and early '80s because companies could write off 100% of these expenses as tax deductions as a way of forging business relationships.

Once the Tax Reform Act of 1986 rolled around, though, the government tightened its leash on companies, and suddenly, only 80% of business expenses could be written off. Actual business had to be discussed by those in attendance, and anything deemed "lavish and extravagant" no longer qualified.

In 2017, practices changed even further when Congress passed the Tax Cuts and Jobs Act, which completely took away the entertainment allowance, cut business meal write-offs to 50%, and put more restrictions on what defined business-related expenses.

Something interesting, however, happened last year when a new law was passed: the Consolidated Appropriations Act of 2021, a piece of controversial legislation pushed by Trump as a way to stimulate the economy following the pandemic.

Now, for the first time since the mid '80s, all forms of business entertainment are once again 100% deductible until January 2023, when the economic crisis is expected to end.

While it may be only a two-year experimental window, just long enough to help restaurants and bars as they reopen, it will be interesting, from a taxpayer perspective, to see what percentage the write-offs revert back to following this flashback to the past. Stay tuned.

Dick convinced me that what he needed was not another salesman or person to manage their day-to-day activities. Rather, he needed someone who could develop a market strategy and coordinate its execution with the distributors and direct salespeople. That manager would have to ensure we were driving growth.

I understood that but was still concerned about how I would be viewed and accepted by those on the sales team. Even though I had a good relationship with each of them, they might be wary of me as their leader.

My approach was to learn from them and then try to add value to their work. Hopefully, I could then make their jobs easier and keep them focused on what they did best—selling.

Just as I did with our distributors, I decided to travel and spend time with each of them. I was committed to learn more about their territories and what they thought would grow the business. Mostly, I wanted to know what they'd like to see improved to make them more effective.

From there, I developed a list of sales targets I could assist with. Depending on the situation, I would help coordinate customer and new business activities with the engineering, quality, manufacturing, or finance departments, as well as other areas.

I also developed specific project plans and actions that were the key to closing business in each territory.

After we got the business, I would track the new orders for a time until I saw the process going smoothly.

Gain Trust First

After a while, I could tell that the sales team respected and valued what I was doing. This allowed me to now make suggestions in areas where I thought we could do better. I usually did this in the form of a question, such as, "What do you think if we approached this customer about using our product for this application like customer X did?" Or, "Maybe the next time we are together, we could go see that customer we used to sell a lot of product to but who hasn't ordered much lately?"

Most of the time, they agreed with me. But sometimes they pushed back, and I respected that. I was fortunate to work with an experienced professional sales team. By earning their respect, I became a more effective manager and received their cooperation and support.

From them, I also learned about selling—still an area I needed to improve. By organizing our projects and managing the steps to completion, we became a focused team, which resulted in strong sales and gross margin growth.

...

During this time, I was working long hours, traveling frequently, and constantly thinking about improving the business. This intense schedule badly affected my personal life.

Recognizing our marriage was in trouble, my wife asked for a divorce. She knew we had grown apart. We had married young and gone off in different directions as we had developed as individuals.

We still had in common the responsibility of raising our kids, though. To do this, we needed to forge a different, more productive relationship. We decided on an amicable divorce and, to her credit, that was how we handled it.

We also decided that, until our boys were grown, we would both live in the same area, share custody, and do our best not to let our choice affect the kids.

I knew not being able to relocate could affect my ability to advance. That, added to the fact that I didn't have a college degree, was something I needed to overcome.

But the most important thing was to make sure the boys had a stable, consistent environment, and that's what we set out to accomplish.

...

I continued making progress as SEMCO's national sales manager. I was reading weekly and thinking more broadly about how the world around me affected both society in general and our business specifically.

During the late 1970s, we were living in a period of stagflation, malaise, and unsettling foreign events, including the Iranian hostage crisis and OPEC-led oil shortages.

Nonetheless, during the four years in my commercial management roles, sales at SEMCO nearly *doubled*—growing from $6.5M to $12M.

By 1982, I was in demand in other parts of the company. I was offered a new position as assistant sales and market manager for our aerospace sealant business. I was told this move could lead to becoming vice president of sales for that business line. The current VP was approaching retirement, and selling aerospace sealants was becoming the largest business in the corporation.

After discussing this opportunity with Dick, I accepted the position as a new challenge.

It turns out, I was selling my way up the ladder.

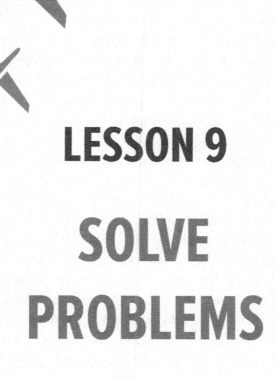

LESSON 9

SOLVE
PROBLEMS

When solving problems, dig at the roots
instead of just hacking at the leaves.
—Anthony J. D'Angelo

There's an analogy between driving a car and leading an organization, when you think about it. Both require looking ahead to avoid risky last-minute maneuvers.

When driving, you're expected to continuously scan the road ten to fifteen seconds ahead of your vehicle and sometimes twenty to thirty seconds ahead if you follow defensive-driving rules for high-risk conditions. That's almost half a mile on the freeway or two to three blocks for city driving.

Many drivers, however, focus only five to eight seconds ahead, and even people who've been driving for a long time get sloppy and overly confident in their abilities. The result? A lot of swerving and crashing.

I still remember what my high school driving instructor drilled into us: "Aim high in steering and leave yourself an out."

It makes sense like the old adage does about seeing beyond the tip of one's nose. If you only stare past the hood of your car, you're likely to get into an accident. You need to look up and out into the future to anticipate what other drivers might do and to plan for the pedestrians, rolling balls, leaping dogs, and swinging doors that come out of the blue. Hazards like these give little time to react, and every second counts.

It's a cautionary tale on short-sightedness that applies to business, too.

Proactive Problem Solving

There are essentially two ways to respond to a problem: reactively or proactively.

Being able to see storm clouds on the horizon is one of the facets of a great leader. You want your management to be the kind of people who service their cars regularly and watch the weather channel nightly so they know when to shut the windows.

With events moving at top speed these days, companies need problem-solvers more than ever. These are the people who not only keep their eyes open but keep their minds open, too.

An idea called the experience trap suggests, essentially, that relying too heavily on past information can lead to preconceived notions that block the flow of new ideas. This trap can leave longtime leaders stagnant and clinging to old views and biases.

The opposite of that is what some call a growth mindset, which is a way of embracing constant learning so you see the bigger picture.

Young people are good at this constant learning. Understanding that not everything is logical or linear helps them embrace the synchronicities in life.

In this chapter, I tell a story about the advantages I had being the new young executive. Namely, I didn't have predetermined answers. I was open to the possibilities that our product wasn't superior and that our competitors could teach us something.

I started with a bunch of questions and followed the research until solutions presented themselves. I really wanted to understand the problem, so I wasn't protecting any ideas in my head, which means I didn't have to lie to myself about what was coming. I could shift perspective and see issues from other people's shoes, letting the evidence guide me to an honest analysis.

Once I saw the problem—which was driven by our poor service, a competing product, and changing market trends—I was able to describe how and why it was happening using customer feedback and statistics.

Basically, we weren't adapting accordingly, and because we hadn't intervened early, the problems were getting worse.

Just as in driving, problem solving in business sometimes requires speed and swift actions. When leaders get caught up in what they learned decades ago, they become short-sighted, much like a driver looking only seven seconds ahead. The one seeing twice as far into the future will be able to better adapt to the ever-changing scenes around him.

Getting people to believe my assessment and see things from my point of view required the use of facts and some salesmanship, but I did it.

After presenting multiple solutions, I was able to persuade those above me of the merits of pursuing what would become the first acquisition I was a part of.

Putting Out Fires

Alonzo "Knobby" Knorbom had been a marine fighter pilot in World War II and Korea. He had leadership presence and was bigger than life. As VP of sales and marketing for our aerospace sealants division, he was head of the company's largest business.

Knobby was an old-school sales leader with an experienced team made up mainly of WWII veterans along with a few younger guys. He was well liked in the company and by our customers, and he had a thirty-year record of success.

Known as a customer guy who mainly liked to be in the field visiting customers with our sales team, he was less interested in business planning and analysis.

At the time, our business was down compared to previous years, and we feared our competitors were taking market share from us.

While still the largest supplier, PRC had some key patents on critical products ready to expire. We did not have much in the way of new products in the pipeline to take their place.

Aerospace sealants are highly technical in nature and must meet highly exacting specifications. For both military and commercial jet planes, their applications included sealants for assembling integral fuel tanks in the wings and sealants for fuselage pressurization and corrosion protection.

I was asked to analyze the market and competitors and also visit key customers. Then, I would make recommendations to Knobby and Dean and suggest a new growth plan and strategy based on our current market position.

After examining sales and margin history by product, I saw that our margins were shrinking and our sales growth was declining in some product lines, especially those in which the patents had expired in the past couple of years.

I then visited our key customers to find out how they felt about our products and service.

In addition, I had long conversations with our sales team and our product development team in the research and development lab.

From my earlier position in the PRC customer service department, I was already familiar with our poor customer service reputation. This poor service created relationship problems with customers, who could not do much about it in the past. PRC was simply the sole source of many products that had patent protection.

In short, this was the first opportunity in a long time that our customers had product alternatives—not options for every one but enough to give us concern.

Now the facts were clear. We were losing market share because of our poor delivery, variable quality, and high pricing. As a result, our sales team was spending too much time firefighting.

Plus, many customers were not as open to evaluating our products for new applications as before. They had no problems with our sales team, but they didn't trust the company. And the teams themselves were becoming demoralized from operational problems.

Even more troubling, one competitor's product used a different curing mechanism than ours.

Our sealants consisted of a polysulfide synthetic rubber in a paste form along with a separate curing agent. These two components were mixed just prior to application to start a chemical reaction that cured the polysulfide paste into a cured rubber.

Our system used a dichromate curing agent that our company had patented two decades earlier. To get around our patent, our closest competitor used manganese dioxide (MnO_2) as a curing agent.

We always believed our system was superior, as it worked well in a wide variety of temperatures and humidity due to manganese dioxide being sensitive to these factors. But customers told me that, in practice, the MnO_2 worked well in their big factories and could be tailored to the needs of all their plants.

So, for instance, in a plant located in a city like Seattle with moderate temperatures and humidity, the reactivity of the MnO_2 could be tailored for that environment. Likewise, in areas with high temperatures and low humidity like the Mojave Desert, the MnO_2 could be tailored for that as well.

That's the approach our competitor was taking to overcome our apparent advantage with the dichromate curing agent. We also found the MnO_2 could be made reliably and consistently.

In addition, our competitor was being aggressive with pricing and, in some cases, selling below marginal costs. Because of that, most of our customers were testing this competitor's sealants.

We needed to act quickly to counter the threat of losing certain customers.

Ironically, we had developed a full line of MnO_2-cured sealants a few years earlier but were so convinced of the superiority of the dichromate system, we had not widely introduced them.

In talking to the R&D team, I learned that we had developed them because the researchers were concerned we might not be able to use dichromate curing agents in the future. These agents were likely to be classified as potential carcinogens by the government's Environmental Protection Agency (EPA) and require special labeling, which might discourage our customers from using them.

In 1982, PRC still led in the US market in these sealants and had a high market share globally. In fact, at the height of the Cold War, they were used on virtually every military and civilian aircraft manufactured in the free world.

The managers responsible for this business (including the company chairman) were the architects of the strategy that had given us this incredible market position.

I knew that persuading them to move away from that successful strategy would not be easy. I was extremely clear, though, that our system had to change as quickly as possible.

Because our competitor was so well positioned to take away market share from us, we had to adjust now to avoid a rapid decline.

And that required support from senior management.

Making a Case

My next step was to write up an overview of the situation and then suggest a strategy and action plan for Knobby and Dean to review.

I had to have solid facts on my side. As the new guy in the business, I was sure I'd be second-guessed. That's why I cited direct feedback from customers and then validated it with the sales team.

If push came to shove, I knew that our salespeople, who had seen the problems themselves in the field, had more credibility than I did.

In my review, I carefully reported the facts and used a situational analysis to describe our current scenario.

Then I offered these three options for evaluation:

1. We could continue to press our current strategy on our existing customers and focus on improving delivery and quality performance. We would only offer MnO_2-cured sealants instead of the dichromate system if the customers insisted.

2. We could decide to make MnO_2 our first choice for new business and proactively work to switch over current customers using dichromate. Over time, this would rationalize the product line into one system and improve delivery and service, but it wouldn't differentiate us from our competitor's system and it would increase pressure on price margins.

3. Or we could acquire our competitor Pro Seal, a division of Essex Chemical, and rationalize our combined product lines based on input from our customers.

My suggestion was bold. I had never proposed an acquisition before, but I felt that it was my job to solve these problems I saw coming at us head-on, and the acquisition felt like a logical solution.

Despite growing and taking market share from us, Pro Seal was really only 15% to 20% of the market. And based on how it priced the products, we did not think Pro Seal was solidly profitable.

However, if we could find a way to acquire Pro Seal, it would set us up to be able to rationalize our product line around MnO_2-cured sealants.

The downside would be that our customers would not be happy with our acquiring their alternative source of sealants.

One thing I knew for sure, though: We needed a new strategy built around MnO_2-cured sealants.

As I expected, I got strong pushback on options two and three from Knobby and the aircraft sealant technical director, who had been executing a strategy of selling the benefits of the old dichromate system for the previous twenty years.

They were reluctant to concede that the products were hard to make reliably and that dichromate was likely to be listed as a potential carcinogen by the EPA.

I received *some* support for selling MnO_2-cured sealants when customers insisted on it, but this would be a limited defensive strategy.

On the other hand, Dean understood the situation and was alarmed at how quickly we could potentially lose market share if we did not act. Not wedded to the existing strategy, he, too, was looking for a strategic option to reverse our current situation.

As it turns out, both Dean and the chairman and CEO, George Gregory, had previously had discussions with the CEO of Essex Chemical Corp.—the owner of Pro Seal—about acquiring all or part of that business. Like they say, great minds think alike.

I'm pretty sure Dean appreciated my suggestions because, shortly after, George and Dean reengaged with Essex's CEO.

And though it took time, they did eventually negotiate an agreement to buy the Pro Seal sealant business from Essex Chemical in 1983.

I think we all felt a little like we had just artfully maneuvered ourselves out of the way of a major head-on collision with reality.

LESSON 10

INTEGRATE IDEAS

Integration is a basic law of life; when we resist it, disintegration is the natural result, both inside and outside of us. Thus, we come to the concept of harmony through integration.
—Norman Cousins

Being able to take the best from opposing worlds and weave them together is an art form, especially in business and particularly in merging together two companies.

You want to hand-pick from both enterprises the best employees, facilities, plans, systems, and overall company missions to, hopefully, create a bigger, stronger, more mature organization.

You have to integrate functions, departments, and managers, making sure everyone is on the same page regarding critical steps and time frames—all while maintaining a low-stress work environment and maintaining productivity.

If it sounds like a nearly impossible task, you'd be kind of right.

The *Harvard Business Review* recently reported that a staggering 70 to 90% of acquisitions fail. That's a lot of fumbled money when you consider the tens of thousands of mergers and acquisitions that happen each year around the world, specifically 49,000 involving almost $4 trillion in 2018 alone.

While the reasons for such failures are numerous, it often boils down to not starting with a tight integration plan from the beginning, full of two-way communication.

And then sometimes, even that's not enough.

Take, for example, the America Online acquisition of Time Warner in 2001. It marked the biggest business merger to date at $165 billion, but then, just a year later, the AOL division imploded and the company reported a net loss of $99 billion.

What happened? The dot-com bubble burst.

Call it poor timing or lack of foresight or even bad luck, but the lesson serves as a good reminder to tread cautiously in the game of mergers and acquisitions. A merger should reduce financial risk, not increase it. To the best of one's ability, you must study market trends and anticipate industry changes before deals are sealed.

I would also add that employees are often at the core of an acquisition's value. They bring with them critical skills, knowledge, and customer relationships that may be irreplaceable.

When merging talent, you want to be mindful not to force too many policies on them at once, and you might want to consider retention bonuses for key players.

When Procter & Gamble bought Gillette in 2005, they gave the Gillette employees a year break from performance reviews. They also formed about one hundred global integration teams, pairing one executive from each company and giving them similar responsibilities so each side felt valued. I like that approach.

I've been through quite a few mergers and acquisitions at this point in my career, so I know all about navigating the emotions that come up from both employees and customers. What I've learned is that transparency is always the best policy.

This chapter covers a stretch of my career in which I played my first role in leading a major acquisition integration, and that's one of the key lessons I learned: Be as forthcoming as you can with information, and people will respect you enough to accept even bad news.

Be clear about the value of the merger, so along the way it's easy to excite and motivate everyone involved, from customers to employees to stockholders. What will be gained? What's the big-picture vision? Is the merger or acquisition happening for greater market share, increased plant capacity, or more diversity in products or services?

Smart, strategic reasons inspire followers and co-creators and prevent internal turf wars.

As Simon Sinek said: "Mergers are like marriages. They are the bringing together of two individuals. If you wouldn't marry someone for the 'operational efficiencies' they offer in the running of a household, then why would you combine two companies with unique cultures and identities for that reason?"

Managing Emotions

When the deal was announced, this news was met with different degrees of enthusiasm within PRC. But it was met with outright alarm from our customers and the employees of Pro Seal.

Knobby and the aerospace sealant management team believed we should close the Pro Seal factory and continue to sell our dichromate sealants while dropping the MnO_2 sealants—as if they had never been in the marketplace. The idea made me shudder.

Our customers were also certain—and highly vocal—that we would raise prices, and then they'd be at the mercy of our poor service.

In addition, the Pro Seal employees believed that we would let them go as soon as the integration of the Pro Seal business was complete.

Dean recognized this deal could be either transformational or disastrous—without much room in between. He wanted to have control over the integration and appointed me to the position of assistant to the president with responsibility for the integration of Pro Seal.

I was excited and honored to be given a lead role in such an important process.

Dean then appointed my old boss, Dick Cude, to corporate vice president for both SEMCO and the aerospace sealant business, with Knobby reporting to Dick.

Among all of us, we set out a clear course of action:

1. We would announce the closure of the Pro Seal plant and move production of the Pro Seal products to our factory in Glendale.

2. We would consult with our customers and let them decide which product line—Pro Seal or PRC—that they wanted us to produce for them in the future.

3. We would discuss the financial condition and low margins of Pro Seal. We would then propose new pricing to our customers, reflecting the value the sealants represented to their applications.

4. We would make sure we kept the best technical and salespeople from Pro Seal.

5. We would work to improve customer service and operations at our Glendale factory.

6. And we would complete the integration by the end of 1984.

With this plan in place, I spent the next year managing and coordinating the integration of the Pro Seal business and took the lead in visiting key customers.

I felt grateful that this deal allowed us to still offer jobs to all of the Pro Seal workers who wanted to come on board with PRC.

With customers, however, our relationship got tense.

Awkward Conversations

When we bought Pro Seal, we found ourselves in the awkward position of having to immediately raise prices. Clearly, our customers didn't appreciate this.

So, we decided to do something we'd never done before. We took a strong approach of transparency and disclosed details to customers that we had never divulged previously.

We did it because it was the right thing to do.

We said, "Look, the numbers don't add up." The direct cost to manufacture the products was almost on par with selling prices from too many years of trying to compete with Pro Seal's undercutting. It was something no company could keep up with.

When you took into account the raw materials, equipment, depreciation costs, manufacturing expenses, and complexities of combined product lines, the profit margins were not sustainable.

We had to show customers that we were creating more value than that, and in the end, our open and honest approach worked.

Customers conceded, and many even walked away satisfied, partly because we had shown them that we cared and we trusted them.

We also promised our customers that we would not eliminate any product lines, and in every case, we offered alternatives to mitigate the price increases if they agreed to change to the MnO_2 product line.

We also showed our customers the value of the combined businesses where we could. That included investing in a larger new product development team and developing new sealants with faster processing times to reduce their costs.

We committed to new product development approaches as well, eliminating lead, chromium, and other suspected carcinogens.

We would also reduce or eliminate the ozone-depleting solvents in our newly developed sealants.

And while we knew that we had the leverage to get price increases in the short term, we also knew that if we did not bring new value and better service to these customers, our strong position would erode over time.

Building New Alliances

Pro Seal had many good people in sales and technical, especially a talented chemist named Ahmed Sharaby.

Ahmed had immigrated from Egypt and was sponsored into the US by his older brother, who was already an American citizen. He had formulated many of the sealants we acquired in the deal and had great commercial instincts. He was the one we made responsible for transferring the Pro Seal products to our factory in Glendale.

Ahmed reported to a powerful research and technology group at PRC and was considered an outsider. He was also highly excitable. This caused friction when he had disagreements with R&D management.

So, many times it fell to me to mediate these disputes, and I most often sided with Ahmed, who was also smart, effective, and fact-based, which appealed to my reasoning.

Like me, Ahmed wanted to grow and develop himself, *and* he loved the business. He and I formed a strong team that complemented each other.

Our shared goal was to make the aircraft sealants business the fastest growing and most profitable area of the company.

Understanding Financial Reports

The weathered 1984 Merrill Lynch pamphlet that still sits on my desk today provided more value to me than any of the business classes I was taking at the time. That's probably because, at thirty pages, it was succinct but thorough. While I can't attach it here in its entirety, I do think half the battle in interpreting income statements is understanding the terminology, so I'm offering some of those definitions here.

Balance sheet: a financial report that shows what a company owns and owes as of a certain date

Income statement: a financial report that compares a company's profit or loss from one year to another

Total current assets: cash, marketable securities, accounts receivable, inventories, and prepaid expenses

Marketable securities: any cash temporarily invested and not needed immediately

Accounts receivable: money due from customers

Inventories: raw materials, partially finished goods, and finished goods

Prepaid expenses: fire insurance premiums, advertising charges, etc.

Deferred charges: similar to prepaid expenses but not included in current assets because the benefits are reaped over years (i.e., new product launches and plant relocations)

Fixed assets: property, plant, and equipment (including office furniture and trucks)

Depreciation: the decline in useful value of assets due to wear and tear

Amortization: the decline in useful value of an intangible that doesn't physically exist, like an aging patent

Accounts payable: money owed to creditors

Notes payable: money owed to banks and other lenders

(continued on page 111)

Accrued expenses payable: money owed in wages, salaries, pensions, attorney fees, and insurance premiums

Debenture: bonds backed by the general credit of a corporation

Working capital: AKA current assets: total current assets minus total current liabilities

Current ratio: current assets divided by current liabilities

Net sales / Operating revenue: money received from customers for items sold or services provided

COGS: cost of goods sold

Operating profit: net sales minus operating costs

Net profit / income: money left after all expenses, including federal income tax and interest income

Operating margin of profit: operating profit divided by net sales

EBITDA: earnings before interest, taxes, depreciation, and amortization (used as an indicator of overall profitability)

Connecting Dots

My role as assistant to the president was a developmental position, and I was actively mentored by Dean. To continue developing my strategic management skills, he asked me to attend a twelve-month weekly evening executive management program at UCLA's Anderson School of Business.

In addition, with the advent of more sophisticated technology, our management reporting systems now provided profit and loss (P&L) statements to individual business unit leaders.

Previously at PRC, the only available information for running the business included sales and costing reports.

I had no idea how to read or interpret a P&L statement, and it bothered me. I was starting to wonder, would this deficiency hold me back?

Then one day, I was sitting at my desk when an accountant from Merrill Lynch, Pierce, Fenner & Smith stopped by and gave me a pamphlet titled "How to Read a Financial Report." I suppose that Dean or Dick had sent him over.

Anyway, the pamphlet was a primer on the basics of reading and analyzing a P&L statement and a balance sheet. This training ended up proving invaluable to me, and to this day, I still have that worn-out pamphlet sitting in my office.

And while I did find the UCLA program I attended to be a great learning experience, surprisingly, the little pamphlet had *more* effect on my career and development in running a business.

It helped me realize that the key was to read between the lines of the P&L and balance sheet and then to connect them to other operating metrics in order to identify areas of improvement.

Business might be all about connecting the dots, but first you must understand the dots.

•••

In 1984, I met a lovely young woman, Penelope "Penny" Peña, at the opening day of the 1984 Summer Olympics in Los Angeles. It was love at first sight, and within a year we married.

All in all, 1984 was a very good year that set the stage for my future—more than I could understand at the time.

LESSON 11

CREATE THE CHANGE

Movements of people create change—
not just any one person or organization, but when lots of
people are in motion around a shared vision.
—Ai-jen Poo

Peter F. Drucker probably said it best when he suggested that "the most effective way to manage change is to create it."

Change is like the law of energy. It is neither created nor destroyed. It transmutes, but it never stops coming. That means we need to harness change the way a surfer rides waves—by instinct and setting ourselves up right.

Nature teaches us this lesson about constant change through seasons and the way different species adapt genetic variations for reproductive success, like soot-colored moths matching tree bark so they don't become bird food.

When we learn to dance with change and not be afraid of it, we learn how to sense its arrival in advance so we can prepare ourselves accordingly and initiate the process of adjustment that circumstances demand. If done well, it will give you more control over your future.

Think of change like a runner in a relay race. The receiving runner begins the process of running before the baton is handed off because the inevitable transition is then more seamless. You have to already be in motion when the change hits or else you're at risk of being destroyed like a brick wall.

Create the Change or Perish

We live in a dog-eat-dog world, especially in business, and the hot mess of industry giants that couldn't adapt in time— think Enron, Woolworth, Compaq—not only paved the road to success for others but sometimes became the dog food.

I'm thinking specifically of the Blockbuster debacle. Theirs is a cautionary tale of epic fumbling from inaction and the inability to adapt in the digital age, and is riddled with karmic irony.

See, in the early '90s, Blockbuster Video had a monopoly on home entertainment and was opening a new store every twenty-four hours, but they were also abusing their customers with late fees.

In the year 2000, Blockbuster raked in $800 million from late fees alone—a whopping 16% of their total annual revenue—and by 2004 they had a $5 billion market value. And a lot of pissed-off customers, one of whom was Reed Hastings, who in 1997 was charged $40 for returning *Apollo 13* late.

What did he do? He created Netflix, a DVD subscription service to compete with Blockbuster.

Just ten years later, in 2007, Netflix began to *outperform* Blockbuster, thanks to its visionary video streaming services.

Then it happened. Only three years later, in 2010, Netflix brought the retail giant down. Blockbuster filed for bankruptcy with an astonishing $1 billion in reported debt. Netflix, on the other hand, can proudly boast a market value today of more than $230 billion.

If that didn't pull on your heart strings, consider this: Blockbuster was approached to buy Netflix in 2000 for $50 million. They declined.

(Pause for a moment to grieve for Blockbuster.)

The lesson? Look for the storm clouds. That's how you know when to close your windows *and* when to invest in wind turbines.

The first step is always recognizing the need for change—*anticipating* the need—whether that change is adapting to evolving consumer habits or setting right the wrongs of the past, like penalizing customers too much for too long.

Watch That Forecast

These days you can get a certificate from Cornell University in change management and study how to navigate power relationships and develop persuasive negotiating skills. Or you can just do what I did and show up every day with an open mind and act accordingly.

In this chapter, I cover a phase of my career in which so much happened so fast that I truly had to rely on my instincts to keep one step ahead of industry changes, global changes, and internal company dynamics to become more efficient, productive, innovative, and profitable.

During this period, we developed new products, licensed new technology, reformulated existing products, negotiated deals, bought distributors, integrated companies, and consolidated or expanded operations for numerous international locations.

I had to redefine my ever-changing role in the company week by week. I did that by making myself as valuable as I could in each opportunity that presented itself.

I *created* change—lots of it.

Career Advances

In August 1985, Penny and I married. Beautiful, smart, and independent, she worked as a legal assistant at a law firm on Wilshire Boulevard and became stepmom to my two boys, ages six and eight.

Penny knew from the beginning that she was taking on a lot. She acknowledged that my job would require me to travel, as I was focused on building my career. From the start, she was and continued to be incredibly supportive.

Not long after Penny and I married, Knobby announced his retirement after more than thirty-five years of service. He was a legend and universally admired for his service as a marine fighter pilot during WWII and the Korean War, and for his great family and excellent leadership at the company.

With Knobby's retirement, Dean, who had been recently promoted to CEO, appointed me as Knobby's successor for VP of sales and marketing in the aerospace and defense products business.

These were big shoes to fill, but I had learned the business through my work integrating Pro Seal. That experience helped me to gain the confidence of those reporting to me *and* to build credibility with our key customers, Lockheed, Boeing, McDonnell Douglas, Rockwell, and Northrup.

Dean also brought in a new executive to the company as vice president of our industrial sealants business. I understood that in doing so, Dean was setting up a potential future successor as CEO. The new executive had come from General Electric, so at that point, I no longer saw myself as a potential candidate for the job.

That said, I still had a challenging role and felt that anything was possible if I could show results and continue to grow the business that I was responsible for.

It was time to focus on the opportunities in front of me.

Expanding Our Influence

With our Pro Seal acquisition integrated, we turned our attention to developing a long-term strategy for the business.

Over the previous year, I had visited all the key customers globally and had discussed with them long-term trends in the aerospace and defense industry.

With this information, we developed a set of objectives for developing new products to address their goals of reducing weight, increasing production efficiencies, and eliminating hazardous chemicals.

We were determined to meet the needs of the next generation of commercial and defense aircraft. To do this, we created the aerospace and defense business plan around developing new products, improving service, and increasing quality performance.

A major change was to adopt a service strategy in which we'd more closely cooperate with our SEMCO distributors to repackage and deliver our sealants. That would dramatically improve our service levels.

This hub-and-spoke approach focused on producing five-hundred-gallon batches of sealants in our large mixers in Glendale. They were then packaged into fifty-five-gallon drums and shipped to key distributors located close to key customers in Seattle, Dallas, Atlanta, New Jersey, St. Louis, and Wichita.

These distributors would then repackage the sealant into three-ounce and six-ounce application packages. From there, they'd directly deliver the packages weekly (and sometimes daily) to our customers' production lines.

All of this was coordinated and supported by our field technical sales team.

To increase the speed of product development, we promoted Ahmed to R&D director—Aerospace Sealants, a position that made him a key player on my executive team.

Ahmed and I continued visiting key customers and developed a set of product development plans and performance targets with each of them.

Then Ahmed and his R&D team set about developing a new generation of lightweight, fast-cure, and environmentally friendly aircraft sealants.

At the same time, one of our large defense customers approached us with an opportunity to license technology it had developed around low-observable coatings used to avoid enemy radar. The customer was having problems with product stability during storage, which made using the product difficult to commercialize. Our technical team persuaded the customer's decision-makers that we had the expertise to solve the problem with a new formulation and the capability to manufacture it.

We negotiated a deal to license the technology and entered into a supply contract that took effect on the approval of our improved formula.

We also assigned Carl Kay, one of our most senior R&D managers, to lead a team in reformulating and qualifying the coating, and then we set up specialized manufacturing and quality labs in a separate and classified area.

Carl's team completed the project and had the coating in production in less than a year.

Over the next two years, we would develop and launch a whole new generation of fast-cure and lightweight sealants and low-observable coatings.

Acquiring More Partners

Meanwhile, our new hub-and-spoke service strategy was working well, resulting in strong sales and growing profits.

Dean Willard became the first to recognize this. He wanted to keep growing by acquiring our aircraft sealant licensee in Newcastle, England.

Integrating Family-Owned Businesses

Family-owned businesses can be lucrative investments. They average 6.65% greater return on investment (ROI) than non-family-owned counterparts, according to a survey of S&P 500 businesses conducted by the Conway Center for Family Business. However, only 30% make it to the second generation, making succession issues and exit strategies critical for those looking to retire or diversify wealth.

That's a lot of opportunity for business acquisition, especially given that more than 90% of firms in the United States are family owned.

Just be aware that buying and integrating family-run operations comes with unique challenges. In some ways, they're the hardest businesses to acquire.

Here's some advice on handling this kind of takeover:

Do your research. Do your due diligence to identify and define risks and opportunities. Family-run businesses might be inefficiently run or digitally challenged, or they might be so entrenched in family politics that interpersonal dynamics have hampered the business. Have a strong understanding of their business and industry beforehand.

Court the family. More than the highest price, it's the long-term agenda of the new management that appeals to these businesses. They want to be sure the family's best interests are at heart, that their shop will be viable after the transaction, and that their employees will have jobs. Show that you are sensitive to their culture, reputation, and social attachment to the community. Build trust by asking for introductions to their longtime customers. Articulate how the company could have a viable future under your leadership.

Be patient. Emotions can run high when it comes to legacies. So much time, money, and energy get put into a family venture, especially if it's been in existence for generations. Family-run businesses tend to be more financially conservative, and if there are numerous family members involved, it can take time for everyone to be in agreement.

Involve a third party. Family-owned businesses tend to be more flexible and less rigid day to day, but don't let those relaxed

(continued on page 121)

practices cut corners in the sale transaction. Documentation must be on point with signed agreements from all the owners, not just the primary. Before striking any deals, find a banker or independent business appraiser to advise during the process. Remember, they may sell only one company in their lifetime, and you are coming from the perspective of buying many companies.

Plan together. To avoid stepping on toes, spend time figuring out what kind of relationship there will be with the family or previous owners and managers after the merger. It's a good idea to solicit the help of the acquired company in drafting the integration plan. That way, everything is agreed upon from the get-go.

This licensee would provide us with our first directly owned manufacturing and R&D laboratory outside of North America. It would also position us well to take advantage of the growth of Airbus Industries and European defense industries.

Happy with those results, Dean decided to also acquire our added-value distributors and further develop our hub-and-spoke service model.

I worked with Dean and others to accomplish the M&A strategy and became part of the team that negotiated and integrated the deals.

In addition to acquiring our licensee in the UK, we bought our distributors based in Los Angeles, Dallas, Seattle, Atlanta, and New Jersey. Under Dean's watchful eye, I got to lead the negotiations for two of the five distributor deals.

I was learning the basics of negotiating M&A contracts, doing due diligence, and integrating businesses.

During this period, I had performed well, but the potential successor from General Electric, on the other hand, did not deliver the results expected from him. So, he left the company.

His departure was a turn of events I had not expected, but it was fortuitous for me.

I still did not think that I was or would be considered a potential CEO successor, but I continued to work hard to develop my skills and tried to put myself in the best position possible—because you never know.

LESSON 12

ADAPT

It is not the strongest of the species that survives,
nor the most intelligent. It is the one that is most
adaptable to change.
—Charles Darwin / Professor Leon C. Megginson

"Over the next decade, we will experience more upheaval and create more wealth than we have in the past 100 years."

That's the prediction from authors Peter Diamandis and Steven Kotler in their new book, *The Future Is Faster Than You Think*. In it, they explore the science behind converging technologies and how this moment in time will reinvent every aspect of our lives, from health, food, finance, and education to transportation, entertainment, and retail. We are, they propose, about to enter a world uncharted and reimagined.

The rapid developments in technology, automation, and artificial intelligence have made the future unpredictable as instantaneous communications continue to shape a culture that just doesn't stop changing. As a result, there's more movement in the workforce and greater market transparency.

In fact, the typical organization today goes through five major firmwide changes in just three years, and the World Economic Forum predicts that over a third of work skills important today will become largely irrelevant in the future.

Likewise, half of executives believe that at least one in five roles in their company will cease to exist in the next five years, according to the 2018 Global Talent Trends Report.

The future is scary and exciting. To survive it, we must have our fingers on its pulse. What we've done in the past is unlikely to be successful in the future.

Sometimes companies need to molt their outside skins the way a snake does. If they don't transform, they die.

In the previous chapter, I suggested that you *create* the change before it hits you; here, I'm offering up that sometimes that's not possible. Sometimes change simply overtakes you—like an uncontrollable merger—and you just have to work with it.

The ability to adapt to change is one of the skills most frequently cited in what makes managers successful.

As major market shifts get faster and faster, leaders must, more than ever, be flexible, emotionally intelligent, and visionary.

While all this seems overwhelming and perhaps even terrifying to some, we must remember that change is inevitable and then do our best to not only anticipate and manage it but embrace it with optimism.

Look for the silver lining, as they say.

There is an old Chinese proverb that goes, the wise adapt themselves to circumstances as water molds itself to the pitcher. I guess you could say I was metaphorically surfing the waves coming at me.

Enter Courtaulds

By 1988, PRC had grown to $110 million in sales, making us an attractive acquisition target for companies such as 3M, Dow Chemical, and others that expressed interest.

George and Dean had had many discussions with interested parties but had a very high valuation in mind.

Early in 1988, Courtaulds PLC, a London-based diversified textiles, coatings, specialty materials, chemicals, and fibers business, acquired 15% of PRC common stock.

That made them subject to a standstill agreement unless they made a tender offer for the rest. This more or less put PRC in play for a takeover.

We waited to see if another company would engage or if we would receive a tender offer for the balance of PRC stock from Courtaulds.

Then, one Sunday in late 1988, the senior executives of PRC were summoned to a meeting at our headquarters. When we walked into the conference room, we were greeted by Richard Lapthorne, CFO of Courtaulds. Dean introduced him and let us know that Courtaulds was making a tender offer for the rest of PRC. That was scheduled for Monday

Tender Offers

To tender is to sell, so logically, a tender offer is a formal offer of money to purchase a publicly traded company. It can also refer to a bid for a project for a branch of the government or a financial institution.

In the world of business, specifically, tender offers are a process that public companies sometimes use to acquire each other.

Typically, one company, or group of investors, interested in buying another will begin by purchasing a small portion, say 10%, of that business as a first step. They can even go as high as 15% and remain incognito.

But once a group shows interest in buying more than 15% of the shares, things turn public, per the law. This is to prevent nepotism and bribery. The process is intentionally very transparent and typically advertised through the newspaper, and in addition, shareholders are contacted directly.

A public notice will invite all shareholders of a corporation to offer up their shares of stock for purchase. The offer will state the purchase price, how many shares are requested, and a deadline for responding.

Having made a public play for the company, the potential investors now have a reason to converse with the CEO and shareholders to try to hammer out a strategy.

Of course, the offer only sets the company into play, as there are no guarantees in life. It becomes a signal to other companies as well: Now is your time to make an offer if interested.

To make sure that laws and deadlines are met, potential bidders may even hire a company that offers tender services. Because, you know, business begets more business.

morning. This action would signal to other interested parties to act quickly with a better offer or let Courtaulds complete the tender offer.

In 1988 Courtaulds was at a crossroad with sales of over $5.9 billion and 57,000 employees operating in textile and industrial businesses in thirty-eight countries. Sir Christopher Hogg, the chairman and CEO, and his team were in the process of positioning the company to demerge the textile and industrial business, as it was thought that each could grow faster on its own.

Part of the plan was to add to the industrial business, which was a diversified portfolio of downstream fibers, films, and chemicals businesses—commodity products that made up more than half of sales (coatings, packaging, and specialty products making up the rest).

Lapthorne was a big supporter of acquiring downstream businesses, which handle the final stages of the manufacturing process and tend to be less capital intensive and more technically driven.

He was given direct responsibility for acquisitions in the US that fit that profile of driving future growth and reducing dependence on low-margin commodities. PRC fit the bill.

So, we were bought.

By the end of the year, PRC was a wholly owned subsidiary of Courtaulds and the company's largest acquisition since their takeover of International Paints in 1968.

The price tag: $260 million—a very high valuation, about 17 times EBITDA (a measure of profitability).

They priced high to ensure that they got the deal. It was a strategic move that put a lot of pressure on PRC to perform as a key new part of their industrial portfolio. It was also thought to be a key piece of Hogg's strategy to position Courtaulds for the planned demerger of its textiles business.

Hogg commented to the press that it was a "crucial step in change of emphasis away from capital-intensive, commodity, cyclical businesses and towards those capable of being differentiated from the competition in many aspects of product and process technology, technical service, marketing, and distribution."

But no matter the reasons, the high valuation made for a great outcome for PRC shareholders.

I had only been in the stock option program for a few years, so my payout was modest compared to the other executives, but it did allow me to buy a larger house at the base of the San Gabriel Mountains, where Penny and I live to this day.

Driving Growth

Managing change was becoming second nature to me, and I easily transitioned into the new ownership structure.

There were not many operational synergies with Courtaulds, or as we call them, SG&As—selling, general, and administrative expenses. However, we had a lot in common with its paints and coatings business called International Paint, which at the time was the largest marine coatings business in the world and sold into many other industrial markets.

Courtaulds decided to run PRC as a separate wholly owned subsidiary but asked us to cooperate with International Paint in areas of mutual support.

Shortly after this acquisition, I was promoted to corporate vice president—aerospace and defense. I would oversee operations, global strategy, and sales and marketing for that division. In addition, I had the responsibility for managing the relationship with our licensees in France and Japan.

The demerger of the textile business from the industrial business was approved by shareholders on March 16, 1990, and the two businesses were named Courtaulds Textiles PLC and Courtaulds PLC.

With PRC now a wholly owned subsidiary of Courtaulds PLC, it now had sales of $2.8 billion. It now had to show that it could grow faster and more profitably on its own.

The next big change for PRC happened when Courtaulds acquired De Soto Inc., based in Chicago.

De Soto was an architectural and industrial paint and coatings supplier. Its biggest and oldest customer was Sears, which *didn't* renew its contract with De Soto.

This put investor pressure on De Soto management to restructure or sell the rest of the company. Management decided to sell, and Courtaulds acquired what was left of De Soto in 1992.

De Soto had an aerospace coatings business that Courtaulds decided to integrate into PRC. I was given the responsibility to lead the integration.

Once it was complete, I was promoted to president and general manager of the global sealants, adhesives, and coatings business with sales of more than $100 million. Rich Giangiordano, a longtime construction products executive, was appointed president of our global construction business unit, which had sales of $40 million. Both Rich and I reported directly to Dean.

Creating Efficiencies

My goal: to drive growth and profitability while achieving market leadership positions in both aerospace sealants and coatings. In other words, find a way to expand *while* reducing costs. It's never an easy juggle.

To improve efficiency, though, we started with the tough decision to consolidate our two UK-based operations into our site in Teesside, UK.

We kept our plant in France to support Airbus in Toulouse, and we set up a service center in Germany to service Airbus in Hamburg.

In the United States, we made plans to close the aerospace coatings plant in Berkeley, California, and move coatings production to our newer plant in Mojave, California. We also made plans to consolidate our global R&D at the research center in Burbank, California.

Expanding Products and Services

We had been in discussions with commercial, regional, and business jet manufacturers to establish a coatings product development plan for exterior coatings and primers. We wanted better performance, environmental compliance, and improved appearance and application.

Our objective: to develop a global product platform for aircraft exterior coatings and primers that could be adjusted to meet the specific requirements of our global aircraft manufacturers.

The platform could be used globally by subcontractors and for airline maintenance. It would meet the most stringent environmental regulations.

To achieve that, we continued to expand the regional distributors we had acquired and rebranded them Application Support Centers, where service could be tailored to customers' needs.

Before long, the changes were working, but we were also beginning to see a cyclical downturn in both the defense and commercial aircraft market. The company's construction business was performing poorly too.

Dean was clashing with his bosses in London over the way forward and left the company for other opportunities in 1994. He had been an important mentor to me and I was sorry to see him leave. Dean went on to continued success as an investor and business leader.

Rising to the Top

After Dean left, Gordon Campbell, a main board director at Courtaulds, became the interim CEO for a few months followed by Colin Ravenhall, CEO of Courtaulds Coatings Australia, for another year.

Their mission was to evaluate the business and management and decide to either bring in another Courtaulds executive, an outsider, or someone within PRC as the next CEO.

During that period, I focused on running my business and getting to know both Gordon and Colin. I gave them my views on what the objectives and strategy should be for the next three to five years and why and how we could achieve those objectives.

They were in a position to recommend the next CEO of PRC, and I was in the running. They wanted to make sure it was someone they had confidence in, both in running PRC and in working closely with the larger paints and coatings business.

They needed someone with a long-term vision for growing PRC and the ability to execute that plan. The new CEO would report to Neville Peterson, a main board director and chairman of the Coatings Management Board.

Neville and the board had responsibility for Courtaulds' global coatings business, which sold over $1.2 billion annually, so the stakes were high.

Then, in 1995, it happened. Almost twenty-two years after I had started as a shipping clerk at the age of nineteen, I was named president and CEO of PRC.

With this promotion, I gained full operating responsibility for a $170 million global business and earned a seat on Courtaulds' Coatings Management Board.

Working hard, adapting, and broadening my perspective had led to achieving results in every position I had held and had earned the confidence of my team and the leaders of the parent company.

I was fortunate to have had great mentors such as George, Dean, Dick, Skip, and Knobby.

I knew my family would be proud. I felt like I had accomplished much more than I thought possible only a few years before.

Now I had the opportunity to prove myself as a CEO.

Calculating the Value of a Business

If you're looking to sell your business or need to know replacement costs for insurance reasons, there are online calculators that can help you figure out your business's value.

Each financial institution has a different approach to valuations, so you may want to try more than one to get an average, but four common approaches are:

- the book value method, which adds up assets and liabilities as seen on a financial report

- the revenue/earnings method, which uses the business's gross income and an industry multiplier to establish a rough estimate

- the discounted cash flow method, which focuses on future performance instead of past financials

- and market comparison, which compares sales prices of businesses in the same industry in your area with similar cash flow

But in general, determining a business's sale price comes down to two factors: the return on investment (ROI) and the relative risk.

ROI is a measure of the net profit since the beginning of the investment, shown as a percentage. In other words:

ROI = (Return / Original Investment) x 100%

If you paid $100,000 for your business and earned $15,000, your ROI would be 15%, for example.

Risk, well, that's more objective and fluctuates greatly by industry. Restaurants and clothing stores are usually considered lower risk than manufacturing and software development.

Risk is also assessed by looking at every aspect of the business. For instance, is there potential for growth? How loyal are the customers? What about the employees and suppliers? Are there tax complications or law suits? Are there established operations and brands in place? The greater the risk of failure, the higher the potential ROI should be.

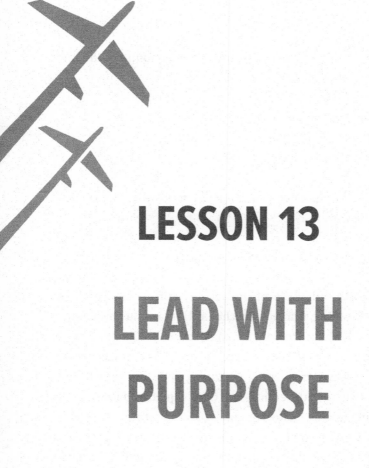

LESSON 13

LEAD WITH PURPOSE

Great minds have purpose; others have wishes.
Little minds are tamed and subdued by misfortunes;
but great minds rise above them.
—Washington Irving

Defining one's purpose in business can be found at the intersection of four circles:

- what the world needs

- what you are good at

- how you believe you can make a positive difference in the world

- and how you can make money

That's the advice from Hubert Joly, former chairman and CEO of Best Buy, who now teaches at Harvard Business School. His Renew Blue corporate transformation became famous for tripling Best Buy's stock in 2013 through his emphasis on big box stores, cherry-picking products, and offering excellent customer care with services like Geek Squad and lowest price matching, giving customers no reason to go anywhere else.

His winning combination was so transformational because it was holistic. It made many different target audiences happy. It gave customers a guaranteed one-stop shopping experience. It increased sales, which pleased employees and shareholders. He even partnered with competitors by creating corners in his stores to showcase products from Google, Apple, and Amazon, which led to increased sales and Best Buy gaining exclusive rights to sell Amazon's smart Fire TV technology.

Basically, he created many win-win situations.

"One of the diseases that exists in this world is the idea of zero-sum games," Joly said in an online interview. "You lose, I win. I win, you lose. That's wrong." The key, he said, is to have a balanced scorecard: "If you focus too much on [the profit], you're actually going to be tempted to do the wrong thing."

I'm with Joly on that. Your reputation in the community, your employee engagement and turnover rate, your long-standing vendor relationships—these are also contributing measures of success.

Pure accounting doesn't take into account things like goodwill. We ourselves must keep tally.

Find Your North Star

In lesson one, I talked about personal purpose, having your own reason for getting out of bed each day, and doing your best to live up to that purpose, be it making a spouse or parent proud or living a life someone else never could, or shaping the world in a way you think makes it better or safer.

Here, we're talking about one's *corporate* purpose, which is a little more specific.

I like Joly's formula for finding the highest mission in one's business. Incorporating the intersection of "making money" keeps the statement real and not unattainable like some abstract goal.

Your purpose should be concise, and it should state what your company does and why it does it. It should be something that inspires each of the disparate groups of stakeholders that you must answer to—the board of directors, the shareholders, your management team, employees, suppliers, distributors, customers, and the communities you operate within, all of which have different expectations for the business.

It's a tall order. That's why you must be crystal clear in your vision. You need to know why you do what you do. Write it down on paper.

Having an aspirational but achievable guiding purpose paves the way in your mind for spontaneous guidance. When we are clear in our intentions, we can respond more intuitively to questions and see our way more easily through the roadblocks and opportunities.

Pass On Your Purpose

Truth is, people get frustrated. They get tired and deflated. Workloads become heavy sometimes and tasks monotonous. People need a guiding light to inspire them. Passion is the fuel that keeps us going.

Once clear in the mind, a leader's powerful purpose must be set loose into the world to excite and motivate others. Your job is to connect the dots and show employees how the small things that they do every day matter and are part of the company's goal. Help people see where they're headed and why.

I experienced a moment recently when I felt like someone needed this. She was the head of human resources at a chemical company where I sat on the board. They were working on a strategy for expansion, and she mentioned how hard it was to recruit young people into an industry that manufacturers chemicals to make plastic.

So, I started asking her questions about her industry, such as, "What do you make? What does it do?" Slowly, I started pulling out of her the answers that sort of solved her own dilemma as she began to understand that her own company was leading the way in creating thinner, stronger plastic, which was in effect reducing the amount of plastic that enters the waste stream.

In the real world, these kinds of incremental improvements are at the heart of sustainability.

Basically, I helped her see the value of what her company does in the context of the world's needs. It's important to understand how we plug into the world around us. How do we treat people? How do we contribute to a sustainable environment?

We're in the world of technology and manufacturing. We're in this to solve problems. We want to be a net-positive for society. We don't just sell stuff and make money.

Once that idea clicked for her, she instantly felt better about developing her recruiting strategy.

That's where a leader shines best, when he or she makes a genuine personal connection that lifts another's perspective higher and reminds them that they're on the right path.

Help people dream bigger.

Big Expectations

Shortly after being appointed CEO, I was at a management retreat near Coventry in the UK, where the top executives from around the world met each year. It was a chance to review Courtaulds corporate strategy, review the businesses in the portfolio, and network.

Each year they had a large, formal executive dinner of about one hundred people or so with the old-school cocktail hour, full dinner followed by after-dinner drinks and cigars, and a speech from the CEO.

It was a slightly intimidating corporate environment, thanks to the formality of the British business culture.

CEO Soft Skills

Here are more management techniques for being an effective CEO:

Take risks. I tend to lean forward rather than backward. The world needs ideological innovation. Think outside the box and set aspirational goals. Try to see things with new eyes.

Let go. Perfectionists make difficult CEOs. Trying to make and control perfect decisions on everything will lead to too much stress on you and your team. Embrace ambiguity and stay focused on your goals, and you will find the way.

Anticipate. Expect the unexpected. Be thorough. Research. Plan. Create an outline of priorities. Could something happen from out of left field to wipe us out? What existential threats are we blind to? You must be honest with yourself and assess where you're at. Mistakes cost time and money. Are you looking far enough ahead?

Adapt. External things happen, be they economic, political, regulatory, or litigious. Every company has challenges. It's part of doing business. Embrace the unexpected and have a contingency plan. Be willing to adjust your plans to get around obstacles.

Reflect before you speak. You always want to think things through before you speak, like who is your audience and what are you trying to communicate? What are you asking for, and what concerns might your listeners have?

Accept responsibility for what goes wrong. Be real and always tell the truth. Be willing to accept the consequences.

Don't second-guess yourself. Bad decisions happen. Get them behind you. Don't oscillate and become gun-shy because of what has already transpired. You need to bounce back quickly. It's the response that matters. Don't become emotionally reactive.

Be an optimist. You must be the beacon of light for others and show them the silver linings. Remain confident and hopeful, but define what's real and don't overpromise.

(continued on page 141)

Borrow from others. Never stop learning. Network with inspirational leaders and try on what you like about their management style.

Leave a legacy. As Warren Buffett once said, "Someone is sitting in the shade today because someone planted a tree a long time ago." What you do should ripple the kinds of consequences you want to see out into the world.

Be articulate. You need to be the big-picture person to pull others from the myopic trenches we all get dragged into. To inspire others, you need to know how to translate complicated ideas into simpler terms.

Be human. Empathize. Share stories. Tell others what happened to you fifteen years ago. I'm not fast to fire people because I know I'm not perfect either. I ask others what they can do better.

In particular, Courtaulds had a policy that a CEO and a member of a management board should have lived and worked in a foreign country as an expatriate.

I had plenty of global experience but had never lived outside of the US. This alone made me a controversial choice with some of my colleagues on the Courtaulds Coatings Management Board. One told me flat out, "You shouldn't have gotten the job." Some on the board could be so opinionated and blunt, very wed to formality over results.

I had been fortunate back at PRC to have been warmly received as CEO. Because I had been there for so long and everybody knew me, I had been the natural, popular choice. The sheer size and profitability of the business I was running alone had qualified me.

But among the unfamiliar faces at Courtaulds, the atmosphere felt different. Like my predecessor, Dean, I was an outsider, and not everyone at Courtaulds had been in favor of buying PRC in the first place.

On top of that, Courtaulds had been disappointed with our performance since they had acquired PRC, mainly because they had paid too high a price and hadn't seen the return on investment they had hoped for.

Dean had taken the heat for this. I didn't want to end up with a similar fate. I could feel the expectations on my shoulders.

Naturally, this being my first year as CEO, I was seated next to Sir Christopher Hogg, the chairman and CEO of Courtaulds himself.

Hogg had been named CEO when Courtaulds was exploding with problems, so he was sort of known at the time for having saved the company.

During the dinner he asked me about how things were going, so I took the opportunity to address the elephant in the room. I wanted to hear about the PRC purchase in his words. What he said stuck with me.

First, he took responsibility. "Look," he said, "don't try to overperform because of our mistake. That's on us, not you." And then he added, "We believe you understand this business. We like your set of objectives. Just do that. It shouldn't affect how you run the business."

Essentially, he told me to focus on my job and everything would be fine.

This advice I took to heart. A ton of pressure was lifted.

Hogg had helped me elevate my vision back to where it should be, just as I would do for that manager in human resources.

Building a Team and Strategy

As Hogg suggested, I focused like a laser beam on doing the things I had promised to do: improving the performance of the business and developing a plan that made sense for its long-term growth through continued investment in R&D and capital investments.

As president and CEO of PRC, my goal was to accelerate growth of our global market in aerospace sealants and coatings.

I aimed to become the market leader in insulated glass construction sealants in North America and return the construction sealant business to acceptable profitability.

PRC became more clearly part of the global coatings business and one of five businesses reporting to the Courtaulds Coatings Management Board.

I would travel to London for board meetings six times a year and, as a member, I was exposed to the other coatings businesses.

I set about developing a cohesive management team, adding:

- A new CFO, Greg Geane, whom we recruited from Nestlé

- David Johnson, an expat from Courtaulds, as corporate controller

- And Rich Giangiordano as president, Insulated Glass Sealants

Several senior executives also retired after Dean left, so I was in charge of those replacements, too. I promoted or hired a number of new senior executives:

- Bill Devlin to vice president of our Global Aerospace Sealants and Coatings Application Support Centers

- Bob Giller, president defense products

- Elliot Stein, vice president operations

- Ahmed Sharaby, vice president R&D

- Dave Morris, general manager SEMCO

- Rob Edwards, managing director Europe

- John Machin, vice president human resources

- Will Fox, also an expat from Courtaulds, as vice president information technology

- And Dick Heimerl, vice president and corporate counsel

I was pleased with the executive team around me, many of whom I had worked with for a long time and who knew the business well. They were all experienced and strong-willed.

If there's one thing I can say about creating your own team, it's to surround yourself with people you trust.

I hire and promote people whose capabilities I believe in so when they come to me for decisions, I can let them make the call. When you hire or promote the right people, train them the right way and empower them from the start; that's working smarter.

Give others the expertise to make the judgment calls you don't have time to make yourself.

Co-Creating a Vision

Together we set the objective to grow to $250 million in sales and developed our strategic plan. When this process was complete, we all shared the exact same vision for the business.

A key part of our strategy was to organize around five growth opportunities:

Aerospace Sealants—sealants that carry out a range of functions, including sealing integral fuel tanks, protecting mating surfaces, maintaining cabin pressurization, and withstanding weathering. To lead this team we appointed Jeff Swindells, global product manager aerospace sealants, and Santo Randazzo, global R&D Lead. Both are experienced leaders.

Aerospace Coatings—coatings used by airframe manufacturers, airlines, and general aviation companies to decorate, protect, and provide corrosion protection and erosion resistance to surfaces. To this team we appointed David Palermo, global product manager aerospace coatings, and Dr. Randy Cameron, global R&D lead, both up-and-coming executives.

Packaging and Application Systems—SEMCO® packaging and application systems used to store, mix, and dispense multiple component and high-performance materials for the aerospace, electronics, and adhesives materials industries

Fenestration Products—sealants used to seal edges of dual-pane windows for high-performance glazing

CEO and the Board

Much freedom comes from being the CEO of a public or private company, but it does have its challenges, and among them is the responsibility to manage the relationship dynamics with the board.

The board of directors is elected to represent the shareholders' interests. The board is a group of people who work together to make sure the investors don't lose money. All public companies must have one consisting of members from inside and outside the company. Private company boards may be family members to boards selected by private equity or other private control investors in companies.

Understanding their roles and responsibilities is a crucial first step for a new CEO. Here's a breakdown.

The board:

- Determines the leadership of the company, appointing the executives and corporate officers such as the CEO, CFO, and/or general manager. This includes recruiting, supervising, evaluating, and compensating them.

- Decides on the organizational structure, along with the CEO, and decides how policies will be governed, typically through monthly or quarterly meetings with the board and the CEO.

- Creates a compensation committee for planning salaries, dividend policies, and benchmarks for executive incentives.

- Determines the company's ideal debt to EBITDA ratio.

- Defines and develops, along with the CEO, the overall business vision, goals, and strategies, including merger and acquisition proposals.

- Reviews financials and potential investments; hires auditors for annual reviews.

- Meets once a year to announce the annual dividend, oversee the election of new board members, appoint key executives, and amend bylaws as needed.

The board of directors doesn't make the day-to-day decisions, but they should stand by close enough to help manage not just the financials but the corporate image and mission integrity as well.

Packaging and Chemical Management Services—
packaging and reselling products of other suppliers

In each growth area, these product managers and technical leaders were focused on driving growth and new product development.

We developed a decentralized accountability culture, where local managers were held responsible for their own business growth and profit and loss.

Our commercial and technical strategy was then supported by a global business model, where our Application Support Centers (ASCs), located near customers, offered differentiated technical services like Coatings Color Matching (CCM), Just In Time delivery (JIT), and Added-Value Packaging (AVP), the latter of which significantly increased sales.

At the same time, we continued to invest in new product development, focusing toward better performance, lower weight, environmental friendliness, and improved efficiency in application.

As a result, we were launching a record level of new products into the markets that we served.

Of course, every scorecard has to be balanced, so the other side of growth is scaling back. We had to do a bit of that, too. We looked for ways to reduce unnecessary fixed costs.

The ASCs were supported by specialized manufacturing centers in the US and Europe, who manufactured the bulk products, as well as by our International Research Center for global product development, located in Burbank, California.

By centralizing production to a few sites and removing complexity, we became more cost-effective, while the ASC network ensured customer service focus.

We also completed the move of our coatings business from Berkeley, California, to our plant in Mojave and consolidated our offsite corporate headquarters back to an office located on our Glendale, California, site.

A lot was going on, but by focusing our key business processes this way, both service and quality improved tremendously.

All of this made us a leaner organization.

LESSON 14

FIND THE BALANCE

Balance is not about something you find,
it's about something you create.
—Jana Kingsford

"There are thousands and thousands of people out there leading lives of quiet, screaming desperation, where they work long, hard hours at jobs they hate to enable them to buy things they don't need to impress people they don't like."

Nigel Marsh said that in his very popular TED Talk on this dilemma. He got a chuckle from the audience, who seemed to agree with him.

The pervasiveness of "work hate" is so heartbreaking for the simple reason that we spend so much of our waking lives working. It makes one wonder.

Me, I've been lucky in that I've never felt that way. I have endured stints when I worked long hours, yes, but it never felt like hard work. It was really just disciplined fun.

I get satisfaction from pushing myself. I like to see where my efforts will take me. I guess that's what they call passion for work.

For many people, though, that's not true.

Author Stephen Covey calls the challenge of work-life balance "without question one of the most significant struggles faced by modern man."

So, how do we tackle this widespread dilemma?

Start by acknowledging what's real.

"Certain job and career choices are fundamentally incompatible with being meaningfully engaged on a day-to-day basis with a young family," Marsh says bluntly. He then warns the audience against "putting the quality of your life in the hands of a corporation."

He makes a lot of somber points for a ten-minute video, but I always like to acknowledge what might be real for some people and then try to put a positive spin on it.

I see it like this: It is up to us to create the lives we want. Life is all about choices. To stay balanced and realistic and not set ourselves up for failure, we have to know what to let go of and when.

Design your own life. If you don't, says Marsh, "Someone else will design it for you, and you won't enjoy it."

That reminds me of a quote by Gustave Flaubert: "Be steady and well-ordered in your life so that you can be fierce and original in your work."

And again, this all goes back to the whys. Have a reason for living and a reason for working, so you're clear about your priorities. It makes handling life's curveballs so much easier.

Marsh also suggests adjusting "the time frame by which we judge our balance," adding, "a day is too short; after I retire is too long."

He finishes his talk with a vision: "If enough people start to set more definitive personal life boundaries, we can change society's definition of success to a more thoughtful and balanced definition of what a life worth living looks like."

I found that inspiring.

But all of that said, what I thought about most after watching that TED Talk was my dear friend Bill.

See, some of us *love* to work. We love the challenge. We love our coworkers. We love the sense of accomplishment we get from our jobs.

There are some of us who would continue going to our jobs up until the very end, if given the choice. I learned this lesson from Bill.

Servant Leadership

There was this essay back in 1970 titled "A Servant as Leader," written by former AT&T executive Robert K. Greenleaf. In it, Greenleaf romanticized a leadership style in which managing people starts with service.

He said a leader should focus on growing his employees as individuals, making sure they're becoming healthier, wiser, freer, more autonomous, and "more likely themselves to become servants."

His inspiration came from a 1932 book by Hermann Hesse called *The Journey to the East*, in which the main character Leo, a servant, disappears and things start to fall apart, leading everyone to realize Leo had been the leader all along.

The bottom line: A truly great leader unites people without ever appearing above them.

From that perspective, I suppose I've had an advantage in some ways. Maybe that's why so many great mentors took me under their wings. I've always been a bit of an underdog. I had to work my way up and learn through the jobs the hard way. Workers can relate to that, and people respect it.

As John C. Maxwell once said: "Leaders must be close enough to relate to others, but far enough ahead to motivate them." So, I guess the advice is, stay grounded but set the pace and keep it up.

Following are some of Greenfield's guiding principles behind servant leadership:

- Listen to others and be open to your own intuition.

- Know when to withdraw and refresh.

- Persuade; don't coerce.

- Accept imperfections and have empathy.

- Conceptualize a clear vision, then implement it step by step.

- Focus more on bettering the people around you than yourself.

And I would add:

- Empower your team; show them you trust their skills; give them authority to make decisions.

- Praise jobs well done in front of others; being seen recharges batteries; small gestures go a long way.

(continued on page 153)

- Help people develop and perform as highly as possible; invest in the coaching, training, and resources your team needs; a CEO's job is to create opportunities.

- Hire people with strong personalities and passion.

- Self-reflect often; a team is only as strong as its CEO.

- Create a light environment; you need a good sense of humor to keep everyone stress-free.

- Roll up your sleeves . . . "A boss says go; a leader says, 'Let's go!'" —E.M. Kelly

- Push your team; have high standards and challenge their abilities.

Remembering Why

We had gelled as a team and everything was going well when I received a call from John, our VP of HR, while I was in Paris on business.

Bill Devlin, our VP of the global ASC network, had been diagnosed with an inoperable brain cancer.

The news was tragic and shocking. Bill was effectively my number two and a popular, effective leader. He was also only in his forties like myself, and he had a wife and three boys.

I was instantly brought back to my feelings as a fifteen-year-old—that familiar anxious pit in my stomach.

When I returned from my trip, Bill and I talked. What had started out as headaches had turned into the worst diagnosis possible. He had been given less than a year to live.

Bill had one stoic request: let him work for as long as he was able to so he could live out his days as normally as possible. He also wanted to spend as much time as he could with his family.

Our whole team was devastated. Bill was like family. I offered whatever support he needed.

Looking back, I realize what an honor it was for Bill to choose to stay on till the end. It speaks volumes about how much he enjoyed his work.

We were a cohesive group. Everybody liked working with each other. We had our serious objectives, but we were also loose at the same time. We had fun.

Bill wanted to be a part of it for as long as he could. That will always mean the world to me.

We did our best to honor his request, though there were times when it was hard not to be overly protective of him as his body succumbed to the fight.

In less than a year, Bill was gone.

Just as my brother had thirty years earlier, Bill showed tremendous courage right up to the end.

I was reminded of *my* why—how each day is a gift that can disappear at a moment's notice.

We need to do what we love, as often as we can, to the best that we can, and while we can.

Bill's loss devastated the team, but like I had to do so many years earlier, we picked up the pieces where we could.

After Bill's funeral, we placed a plaque and held a ceremony in front of our newly built quality lab and administrative offices at our Mojave plant.

Then we began the process of moving on.

As CEO, I knew it was up to me to lead the way.

Learn to Juggle

Having the time to attend to one's emotional, intellectual, and spiritual needs is hard enough with a family; it can get harder at the top. You have to learn to pace yourself so you have the internal fortitude to show grace under pressure.

Being a CEO, specifically, means wearing many hats.

The job is so much more than increasing year-to-year sales growth and returns on investments. You are also responsible for the ethical culture of the company, the internal and external communications, and all inherent risks. You have to drive growth, make sure you don't get sued, and be the person who reassures everyone after major setbacks.

Ultimately, you are responsible for everything. You are both offense and defense, so if you don't manage your time well, it will manage you.

To do all of these things, a CEO must learn to let things go. Stop trying to be perfect because it will never happen.

There's a quote I like by an American businesswoman named Betsy Jacobson. It wisely goes, "Balance is not better time management, but better boundary management. Balance means making choices and enjoying those choices."

There's no time for second-guessing oneself in leadership.

Learn quickly from your mistakes and move on. You must learn to be decisive. Time is money, as they say, and it's true. I don't have the luxury to sit on decisions. I do the best professional assessment I can and then decide. We're in or we're out. I like to keep things moving at a good pace.

Working hard is not about long hours; it's about working smarter. To me, that means making decisions quickly so issues don't build up. Get things off your plate as soon as possible. When too much is happening at once, that's when people feel stress. Stay focused on the key things that will drive the business forward and get you to your goal.

Like Simon Sinek said so well, "Every instruction we give, every course of action we set, every result we desire, starts with the same thing: a decision."

If you're going to make dozens of decisions a day, you have to learn to trust your own judgment and to trust that of the people who work for you. Learn when to let go.

Spend your time on activities that advance your overall purpose by setting priorities and boundaries, and stay guided by a clear mission so you become more purposeful with finite resources like time and energy.

Life-Work Balance

Brian Dyson, the former vice chairman and COO of Coca-Cola, made this analogy about life, and it stuck with me after Bill's passing:

"Imagine life as a game in which you are juggling some five balls in the air . . . work, family, health, friends, and spirit. You will soon understand that work is a rubber ball . . . but the other four balls—family, health, friends, and spirit—are made of glass."

We all have to take responsibility for maintaining the boundaries in our lives and never let one area of our life grow out of control like a weed that suffocates the other plants.

Make sure that you're enjoying your life *while* you're living it.

Taking Stock

After Bill's death, I had the tough task of choosing his replacement. I decided on someone I believed Bill would have approved of.

Some years earlier Bill had recruited Dave Morris—yes, the same Dave Morris that I had met on my first business trip, who at the time was general manager of the John W. Blair company, our distributor in Ohio.

Dave had joined PRC to start an ASC center in Indiana from scratch. At the time United Airlines had invested in one of the largest commercial aircraft maintenance centers in Indiana, and we wanted to set up an ASC center to service their business.

Dave had shown excellent leadership and initiative and had made a great success of it. He had then moved to California to become general manager of our SEMCO business.

I asked him to take on the management of the global ASC network as well and appointed him VP of SEMCO and Application Support Centers.

We all rededicated ourselves to the businesses, kept our heads down, and achieved results.

During next five years, PRC continued to win in the marketplace with our successful new product launches and the implementation of our hub-and-spoke service strategy.

Our accomplishments:

1. We grew to $241 million and $59 million in EBITDA with a compound annual growth rate in sales of 8% and EBITDA of 22% over the five years ending in 1999 and were on track to grow to $250M and $63M in EBITDA in 2000.

2. We achieved our goal to become the clear global market leader in aerospace sealants and coatings.

3. We improved the profitability and market position of our insulated glass construction sealant business in North America.

4. We improved our service and reduced trading working capital from 25% of sales to close to 15% of sales.

5. We became one of two crown jewels in the Courtaulds coatings business portfolio (the other being the marine coatings business).

6. We had developed a high-performance, customer-focused business culture throughout the organization.

I was the leader of a great management team performing at a high level. We had developed good relationships with Courtaulds' senior management, and we were paid well. Life was good.

What more could I want?

LESSON 15

KNOW WHEN TO LEAVE

Regret for the things we did can be tempered by time;
it is regret for the things we did not do that is inconsolable.
—Sydney J. Harris

It's never easy to know when to leave a job, especially one that you've worked so hard to get to.

There are a lot of reasons why people do it, though—from boredom to lack of adequate compensation, strategic or policy differences, or commonly, personality issues with management.

And sometimes it's more complicated than that—not so black and white—but rather a mixed bag of reasons, changes, and temptations. That was the case for me.

Winds of Change

In 1998, about four years after I became CEO, Courtaulds started running into headwinds.

The Courtaulds coatings business was doing well overall, but the cyclical fibers and specialty chemical businesses that made up more than half of sales were having significant performance issues.

In his book *The Rise and Fall of Great Companies*, Geoffrey Owen says of Courtaulds: "The share price was now at a level where the coatings business on its own was worth more than the stock market value of the whole company."

This company low point in the context of the reshaping man-made fibers industry made Courtaulds an attractive target for a hostile bidder.

Courtaulds' senior executives and board of directors decided to demerge the coatings business from fibers and chemicals, operating them as two separately listed public companies.

They made the announcement in 1998, which drew the attention of major specialty chemical player AkzoNobel, who made an offer, and the companies announced the deal.

The demerger was off.

PPG Industries, another global supplier of paints and coatings, followed suit by announcing that it was considering a counterbid for Courtaulds.

After discussions with PPG, Akzo agreed to sell Courtaulds' packaging coatings and the Porter paints architectural coatings businesses to PPG once Akzo closed its acquisition of Courtaulds. Akzo would acquire and then break up Courtaulds with the goal of retaining the coatings business not promised to PPG and selling, or doing a public offering (of equity shares), on the fibers and specialty chemical business.

That left AkzoNobel with one final issue to sort out. Akzo Aerospace Coatings, a division of AkzoNobel, had been our main global competitor in aerospace coatings. During the antitrust review of the proposed acquisition, the European Commission decided that AkzoNobel could complete the deal, but it would have to put PRC into a trusteeship.

AkzoNobel was given a year to either sell its own AKZO Aerospace Coatings business and keep PRC or sell PRC and keep their AKZO Aerospace Coatings business.

In the end, AkzoNobel's board decided to sell PRC.

PPG made the highest bid, and we were sold to them for $512M in October 1999.

This was one month after I had turned forty-six. It was time to think about my future.

Nothing Lasts Forever

When I stepped back to honestly assess everything I had done and created in my twenty-six years at PRC, I was incredibly satisfied.

Wanted: Middle Market CEOs

Large-cap multinational industry giants get most of the media play, along with trendy tech startups, but there's a slew of overlooked companies that sit between those two worlds. In fact, the United States has more middle-market companies than the next fifteen top global economies.

Exactly how many? That depends on who you ask.

Investopedia reports about 200,000 midsize companies and defines them as firms with between $10 million and $1 billion in annual sales, but that's an awfully wide net to cast. A more refined definition would be those with annual sales between $50 million and $500 million, like the ones recently tallied in a massive global survey by HSBC Bank. In this size category, HSBC found about 55,700 American midsize companies with annual sales totaling $1.7 trillion to the US economy. They also support 16.5 million American jobs.

Who are these companies? Over a third of them are wholesale and retail stores, with business services (design, engineering, legal, accounting, etc.) and manufacturing close behind.

Collectively, middle-market businesses function like the backbone of the economy, but individually, they struggle from not being as nimble as smaller firms nor as capable of self-promotion and economies of scale as bigger companies. This is why they often have different kinds of owners, investors, and business theories.

Some other key considerations to keep in mind about midsize companies:

- They are sixteen times more likely to be private than public.

- Midmarket CEOs tend to have more hands-on responsibility and freedom in managing profit & loss compared to CEOs at larger firms.

- Hiring and retaining talent can be challenging due to competition with cash-rich larger firms.

- They tend to have leaner general and administrative costs, and executives tend to wear more hats than large corporations.

I loved my job. I loved leading the team, developing people, and taking calculated risks. I loved the freedom.

People at big firms sometimes complain that we should have done this or that, but we couldn't because management decided it wasn't a priority. That wasn't my case.

I had been fortunate at PRC to have been able to make important decisions thus far.

Being the CEO is liberating. You get to develop forward-thinking strategies to grow the business. I loved looking ahead to make my company more valuable in the future than today.

I loved the travel, too. I must have spent half my time traveling. I had trips where I'd start in Los Angeles and go to Hong Kong, Japan, then Singapore before jetting off to Germany, Paris, and London and then back to LA, all in a couple of weeks.

I've flown more than six million miles on business as of today, and I still love it. I've been to places I might never have seen otherwise, such as London, Frankfurt, Paris, Tokyo, Beijing, Singapore, Sydney, Cairo, Mumbai, Porto, and Madrid, among many others.

Even the small towns were fun to visit because you end up meeting with the local team, who knows how to show you around.

I have friends all over the world, thanks to being CEO of PRC. Traveling has made me more worldly and given me a broader perspective on life.

And, perhaps best of all, I loved seeing the people who worked for me do better than they themselves had thought they could.

I really did love what I was doing. I guess that's what they mean when they say, "Find something you love to do and you'll never have to work again."

But everything has its season, right?

I knew from what I had seen and felt so far under PPG that things would be different now at PRC. More corporate. I also knew I would not be given the same freedom to operate the way that I had for so long.

If I wanted to take a real risk and challenge myself to greater heights, I knew it would have to be elsewhere. I also knew that I was at the right age to make that kind of jump.

Ralph Waldo Emerson once said, "The mind, once stretched by a new idea, never returns to its original dimensions." That's how it felt for me. Once the idea was planted, it grew like a snowball rolling down a hill. I could feel it in my bones. Sometimes, that's the best guidance you have.

Jumping Ship

The intellectual decision to leave was easier than the emotional one, though. I had learned everything I knew about running and leading a business at PRC. I knew almost everyone in the industry, and the employees felt like family to me.

I will always look back fondly on my time there. I owe much to the people who mentored me and allowed me to make mistakes while supporting me and believing in me.

They created an environment that let me rise as far and as fast as my talent would take me. I had earned their trust and support through hard work, initiative, and results.

The simple approach of always trying to do things before being asked had served me well.

I also knew that it was time to get out of my comfort zone and take another risk—win or lose.

I began to put out feelers for other CEO opportunities. It was time to use what I had learned at PRC to take on new challenges.

I've heard it said that once you start thinking about and saying out loud what you really want, a shift happens in your mind and you begin to magnetize powerful reflections of that. I think that's true because things began to happen quickly.

The stories I could tell you about what happened to me after I finally left PRC warrant a book twice this long.

I would go on to not only be CEO of another company but to eventually become co-founder and CEO of a company I started from just a thesis and built through private equity into a global business three times more valuable than PRC.

That is a story you can expect to read soon. Very soon. Say, in six months. Because one of the CEO skills I take great pride in is getting things done.

Mike would be proud.

POSTSCRIPT

As I mentioned in the preface, I wrote this book to inspire others. I wrote it to capture my legacy, to understand for myself, in the looking back, what is this mark I've left behind? Can it help others?

I believe it can.

What makes my success story so relevant and relatable to so many people is that *nothing miraculous happened*. I followed a relatively simple recipe for success: the right connections plus some extra initiative compounded with the willingness to learn, the discipline to solve problems, and the natural knack to adapt and envision the next step—a business cocktail anyone should be able to reproduce.

If you can just be there, be open-minded, be willing, be prepared, and be disciplined, you'll be ahead of the game, relatively speaking. And gains, little by little, add up over the years. You only need to be better than the other candidates up for the job at hand. From there, you set your sights on new goals. I love challenges, so this kind of thinking and process appeals to me.

More than success, though, I hope one of the key takeaways you get from this book is to lead with clarity and empathy in pursuit of shared goals. To remember that life is fragile, it's short, and it should be filled with meaning, even in business. We should not only treat others with kindness and inclusion, but we should remember our place in the bigger picture.

Each person in business should be self-analyzing on a regular basis, asking, "How can I leave the world a better place than how I found it? What, as a team, are we trying to accomplish? What does winning look like? And how can I help my team to grow and develop?"

The acronym LUV stands for listening, understanding, and validating. These concepts are powerful when leveraged with employees. The more validated people feel, the faster problems resolve because motivation increases. People need to feel seen now more than ever. They want clarity, honesty, accountability, and empathy from their leaders.

If leadership is what you strive for, make sure you're doing it for the right reasons. We're entering an age that demands leaders be able to strike that delicate note between leading from the front but not being too far ahead.

Bring people with you. Set aspirational but achievable goals. Listen to your instincts. Take the heat when you lose, and share the credit when you win.

And check out my next book, *Buy & Build CEO— Leveraging Private Equity to Build a Winning Global Business.*

ACKNOWLEDGMENTS

As I rose to more senior levels in business, I began working to pay forward the mentoring I received as a young person learning about business and leadership.

This book is an attempt to do so more widely, to reach more than just those individuals I have had the privilege to mentor over the last two decades.

After writing this story, I spent time finding the right editorial and publishing team to make sure it was a professional effort. I was fortunate to find Barbara McNichol of Barbara McNichol Editorial, Gail Woodard of Dudley Court Press, and Linda Mooney, who have all been instrumental in providing guidance and support in research, editing, improving, and launching this book.

I would not have much to write about if it weren't for the many mentors who took time to teach me the ropes. They include George Gregory, Dean Willard, Richard "Dick" Cude, Alonso "Knobby" Knorbom, Skip Moline, and Danny Iwamota.

Much of my success as CEO of PRC was due to the management team I was privileged to lead, including Ahmed Sharaby, Elliot Stein, Bill Devlin, Greg Geane, David Johnson, Dick Heimerl, Dave Morris, Rich Giangiordano, John Machin, Bob Giller, Carl Kay, Santo Randazzo, Jeff Swindells, Randy Cameron, and David Palermo, as well as so many others.

Finally, I want to acknowledge the love and support of my family. Penny, my wife, took all the risks with me and is my biggest supporter. Thanks to my sons, Mike and Josh; our wonderful daughters-in-law, Deanna and Madeline; and of course our grandchildren, Madyson, Kasee, Calvin, Gibson, and Marlowe.

I hope this book inspires them to follow their dreams as they set aspirational and achievable goals wherever life takes them.

Like most things in my life, this book would not be possible if not for my parents, Eric and Laura Clark, and my brother, Michael Scot Clark. May they rest in peace.

MORE BY TED CLARK

BUY & BUILD CEO

This is a sneak peek into the world of high-stakes, high-rewards business. This is an account of how I came to understand and utilize what "private equity capital" stands for—free market capitalism—and subsequently built, over time, a global business with annual sales of more than $650 million, with 1,500 employees, and an enter-

prise value of $1.6 billion . . . all from just an idea and a thesis.

This is a story about creating wealth—lots of it. Private equity helps democratize access to the American Dream by investing capital in people and companies based on merit and results. At its best, it creates value by partnering with management teams and helping those teams realize their potential.

Come along as I explain exactly how I used private equity support to create significant wealth for my family, my team, and our investors while actualizing our vision and achieving the American Dream.

ABOUT THE AUTHOR

Theodore (Ted) Clark is a businessman, entrepreneur, and investor with more than forty years' experience as a senior executive in both public and private equity-owned specialty chemicals companies.

Starting as a shipping clerk, Ted rose through the ranks to become CEO of two leading adhesives, sealant, and coatings companies. He has invested in and served as a director of four private equity–backed specialty chemical companies and recently retired from chief operating officer at H.B. Fuller Company, a NYSE-listed public company.

Ted currently resides in Sierra Madre, California, with his wife Penny and their two cats, Hope and Faith.

Connect with Ted online at

www.shippingclerktoceo.com

LinkedIn: Theodore Clark